Arabic Voices

2

Authentic Listening and Reading Practice in Modern Standard Arabic and Colloquial Dialects

lingualism

ISBN: 978-0985816063

Cover art: © Jiri Kaderabek/bigstockphoto.com

Photo credits: © jgaunion/bigstockphoto.com (p. 87); © Paul Cowan/bigstockphoto.com (p. 140)

website: www.lingualism.com

email: contact@lingualism.com

Table of Contents

All segments from *Arabic Voices 1* and *Arabic Voices 2*

Segments spoken in dialect are marked with an asterisk (*).

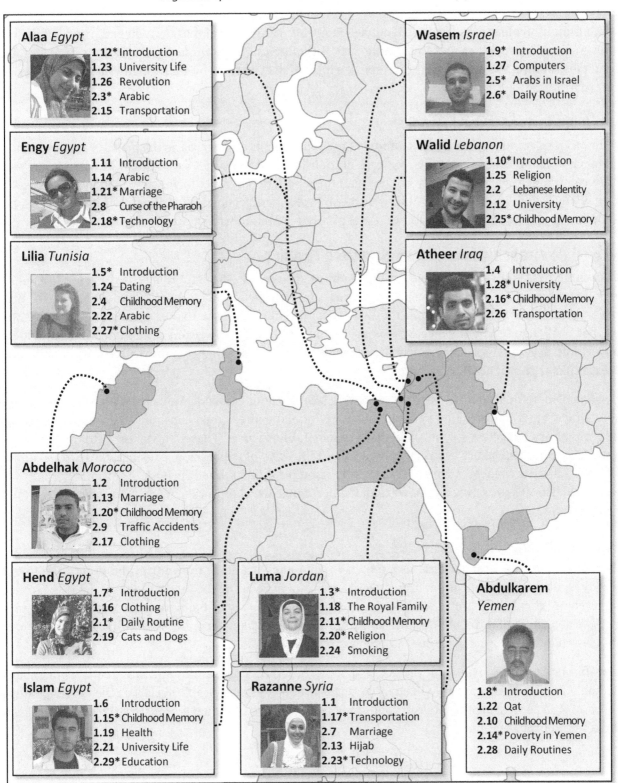

Alaa *Egypt*
- **1.12*** Introduction
- **1.23** University Life
- **1.26** Revolution
- **2.3*** Arabic
- **2.15** Transportation

Engy *Egypt*
- **1.11** Introduction
- **1.14** Arabic
- **1.21*** Marriage
- **2.8** Curse of the Pharaoh
- **2.18*** Technology

Lilia *Tunisia*
- **1.5*** Introduction
- **1.24** Dating
- **2.4** Childhood Memory
- **2.22** Arabic
- **2.27*** Clothing

Wasem *Israel*
- **1.9*** Introduction
- **1.27** Computers
- **2.5*** Arabs in Israel
- **2.6*** Daily Routine

Walid *Lebanon*
- **1.10*** Introduction
- **1.25** Religion
- **2.2** Lebanese Identity
- **2.12** University
- **2.25*** Childhood Memory

Atheer *Iraq*
- **1.4** Introduction
- **1.28*** University
- **2.16*** Childhood Memory
- **2.26** Transportation

Abdelhak *Morocco*
- **1.2** Introduction
- **1.13** Marriage
- **1.20*** Childhood Memory
- **2.9** Traffic Accidents
- **2.17** Clothing

Hend *Egypt*
- **1.7*** Introduction
- **1.16** Clothing
- **2.1*** Daily Routine
- **2.19** Cats and Dogs

Islam *Egypt*
- **1.6** Introduction
- **1.15*** Childhood Memory
- **1.19** Health
- **2.21** University Life
- **2.29*** Education

Luma *Jordan*
- **1.3*** Introduction
- **1.18** The Royal Family
- **2.11*** Childhood Memory
- **2.20*** Religion
- **2.24** Smoking

Razanne *Syria*
- **1.1** Introduction
- **1.17*** Transportation
- **2.7** Marriage
- **2.13** Hijab
- **2.23*** Technology

Abdulkarem *Yemen*
- **1.8*** Introduction
- **1.22** Qat
- **2.10** Childhood Memory
- **2.14*** Poverty in Yemen
- **2.28** Daily Routines

Introduction

Who is an Arab?

An Arab is an individual whose native language is Arabic. Arabic encompasses a diverse range of dialects found across northern Africa and the Middle East. Although there are numerous variations of Arabic, one commonality among all Arabs is that they speak a local dialect as their mother tongue rather than Modern Standard Arabic.

What is Modern Standard Arabic?

MSA, or Modern Standard Arabic, is commonly taught in schools and serves as the primary written form of the language. While Arabs primarily converse in their local dialects, they resort to MSA when it comes to written communication. This linguistic phenomenon, where two distinct forms of the language are used in everyday life, is known as diglossia. MSA is also employed in television and radio news broadcasts, as well as in public speeches, where the Arabic text is typically read aloud from a prepared script.

How well do Arabs speak Modern Standard Arabic?

It is essential to acknowledge that no Arab is a native speaker of MSA, and it is refreshing for learners to recognize that even Arabs themselves do not speak or write MSA flawlessly. While most educated Arabs have varying degrees of fluency in MSA, they also encounter difficulties with the same complex grammatical rules that challenge learners. Since MSA is predominantly used for written communication, individuals often exhibit a lower level of proficiency when it comes to speaking it, particularly in spontaneous conversations without relying on written text.

For instance, individuals may be capable of writing MSA without incorporating elements from their native dialect. However, when speaking spontaneously, colloquial expressions, vocabulary, pronunciations, and even grammatical structures from their dialects inevitably surface. These "mistakes" often occur due to automatism, where speakers are accustomed to certain ways of expression, causing words to be spoken before they have a chance to consider how they should be formulated in MSA. Additionally, there are instances where speakers may be unaware that a particular word or phrase belongs to their dialect and is not part of MSA.

How do Arabs view their dialects?

Arabs widely perceive local dialects, also known as colloquial Arabic, as the natural and practical means of everyday spoken communication. However, there is a prevailing belief that these dialects are not considered as "correct" or "pure" Arabic and are deemed unworthy of being written. When conversing in English, Arabs often refer to their dialects as "slang" and may struggle to understand why a foreigner would be interested in learning a dialect instead of focusing solely on MSA.

The preference for MSA over local dialects is partly rooted in a sense of pan-Arab identity, but religion undeniably plays a significant role in shaping this attitude. Classical Arabic serves as the language of the Quran, and MSA represents the modern adaptation of this classical language, adjusted to meet the demands of the contemporary world.

How is colloquial Arabic written?

Due to the informal nature of dialects, there is no standardized orthography agreed upon by all speakers. While certain popular spellings have emerged over time, there can still be variations in the spelling of specific words. Some individuals tend to adhere closely to MSA spelling, even if it does not accurately represent the pronunciation in their dialect, while others prefer to modify the spelling to reflect the actual pronunciation.

In this book, the former approach has been predominantly followed. This decision aims to assist you, the reader, in recognizing words you may already know from MSA. However, it also means that you will need to pay close attention to discern regional differences in pronunciation.

How can this book help me?

In the Arabic Voices books, you may notice occasional mistakes made by the speakers, and your observations are likely correct. There might be mispronunciations or misuse of words, occasional deviations from grammatical rules, and instances where sentences are left unfinished as the speaker decides to rephrase their thoughts. This can pose an additional challenge for listening comprehension.

However, it is incredibly valuable to encounter authentic, spoken Arabic in its various forms and speeds, presented by a diverse range of native speakers. This aspect is often missing from many course books that tend to focus on carefully crafted, unnaturally slow, and flawless audio recordings. The Arabic Voices series aims to bridge this gap by providing refreshing and natural content that presents challenging opportunities for enhancing listening skills.

By exposing learners to real-life Arabic conversations, including the imperfections and nuances that naturally occur in spoken language, the Arabic Voices series offers a unique and insightful way to improve listening proficiency.

Can I benefit from this book at my level of Arabic?

While Arabic Voices is primarily designed for intermediate and advanced learners, even students at lower levels can derive some benefits from listening to and studying the segments. It is important to note that the goal is not to understand everything comprehensively from the beginning. Depending on your level, your initial understanding of a segment may range from as low as 10% to as high as 90%.

By engaging in exercises and reviewing the accompanying text while listening to the segments multiple times, you can gradually increase the percentage of understanding. The key measure of progress lies in improving your comprehension over time and pushing your language skills to a higher level.

By adopting this approach, the material in Arabic Voices can prove useful for learners across a wide range of proficiency levels. Each learner's focus should be on incremental improvement and the development of listening skills, regardless of their starting point.

How to Use This Book

In order to fully benefit from this book, it is crucial to exercise discipline by refraining from reading the texts and translations before thoroughly studying the listenings. This point cannot be stressed enough. Reading the texts and translations before listening significantly alters the dynamics and limits the potential gains from the listening exercises.

The recommended approach is to first listen to the segment multiple times while actively engaging with the exercises provided in the book. These exercises are designed to help you grasp the main ideas initially and gradually uncover further details as you revisit the listening material. Only after you have comprehended as much as possible through the exercises should you proceed to study the accompanying text and translation.

By following this step-by-step guideline, you can optimize your efforts and maximize the efficiency of improving your listening skills.

STEP 1: SELECT A SEGMENT TO STUDY

You have the flexibility to choose segments in any order you prefer. However, there is a gradual progression from shorter and slower segments to longer and faster segments within each book. To guide your selection, refer to the box on the right side of the segment's title. This box provides information such as the speaker's name, country of origin, the variety of Arabic (MSA or dialect) used in the segment, the number of words in the segment, and the speaker's rate of speech (words per minute).

For accessing the corresponding audio, the MP3 files that accompany Arabic Voices can be downloaded for free from www.lingualism.com/audio. Additionally, the audio can be streamed directly from the website for your convenience.

STEP 2: TITLE AND KEY WORDS

Before listening to the segment for the first time, it is important to read the segment's title and study the key words associated with it. Approaching a listening exercise without any context or knowledge of the topic makes comprehension in a foreign language significantly more challenging. By knowing the general topic beforehand, we can enhance our understanding by drawing on our past experiences, anticipating possible content, recognizing familiar words, and making educated guesses about unfamiliar words and phrases. Familiarizing yourself with the segment's title and key words provides a valuable foundation for effective listening comprehension.

STEP 3: MAIN IDEA

Next, identify the main idea of the segment from the given choices. If you are not entirely confident about the main idea, listen to the segment once more to narrow down your options through a process of elimination. Once you feel confident that you have determined the main idea, check your answer. (The answers for the exercises can be found before the text and translation on the following page.) If your answer was incorrect, listen to the segment one more time with the main idea in mind to reinforce your understanding.

STEP 4: TRUE OR FALSE

Respond to the "True or False" questions provided. Avoid reading ahead to the multiple-choice questions, as some of these may inadvertently reveal the answers of the true or false questions. If you feel uncertain about any of your responses, listen to the segment again before checking your answers. In the answer key, you will notice that most answers are accompanied by a small number. These numbers correspond to the line numbers in the text and translation that provide the answer. If you are unsure why a particular answer is incorrect, quickly refer to the text and/or translation for the corresponding line number. Exercise self-discipline to avoid reading beyond the specified line number. Listen to the segment again and mark a check next to each true or false question as you hear the answer.

STEP 5: MULTIPLE CHOICE

Respond to the "Multiple Choice" questions presented. Follow the same guidelines as for the true or false questions. Note that both the true or false and multiple-choice questions are derived from information found in the segment, based on the information provided by the speaker, regardless of the accuracy of the information. Each question can be viewed as being preceded by "According to the speaker..." or "The speaker mentions that...".

Apply the same self-discipline as before, using the line numbers in the text and translation to check your answers when needed. Avoid reading beyond the specified line numbers. Listen attentively to the segment again and mark your answers for each multiple-choice question as you hear the corresponding information.

STEP 6: MATCHING

Engage in the matching exercise by connecting Arabic words and phrases to their corresponding English translations. The style of matching exercises may vary depending on whether the segment is in MSA or a dialect.

For MSA segments, the focus of the vocabulary is mainly on high-frequency adverbs, connectors, and phrases. Nouns, verbs, and adjectives are usually excluded since the words each learner knows or needs to learn can vary significantly. Later, when you study the text and translation, you can look up specific words you are curious about and wish to learn.

For dialect segments, there are three columns. The middle column lists words mentioned in the segment that differ significantly from MSA. As you may be less familiar with various dialects, make your best guesses in matching these words to their English and MSA translations. Take your time and learn by actively working with the words, avoiding looking up the answers too quickly.

After matching the words and checking your answers, listen to the segment again while checking off the words as you hear them, reinforcing your understanding of the vocabulary in context.

STEP 7: TEXT AND TRANSLATION

Having completed the exercises and gained a better understanding of the segment, you are now ready to move on to studying the text and translation. This part offers more flexibility and allows you to approach it based on your level of Arabic proficiency and comfort with the text.

Here are a few suggested approaches:

1. Cover the Arabic side and begin by reading the translation. Then, attempt to translate the English back into Arabic based on your recollection of the segment.

2. Engage in brainstorming, where you try to come up with possible Arabic equivalents for the words or phrases in the English translation. Afterward, uncover the Arabic side and compare your ideas with the actual text.

3. Alternatively, cover the English side first and listen to the segment again while reading along with the Arabic. You can pause the audio to repeat each line aloud for practice.

In any case, the side-by-side arrangement of the Arabic text and its English translation allows for various self-testing methods. You should be able to match up most words and phrases with their equivalents in English. Consider highlighting useful and interesting vocabulary and phrases that you wish to learn for future reference.

STEP 8: FOCUS

Certain segments in the book may include a dedicated Focus section. This section provides a concise review of grammar points that are exemplified within the segment. When studying the texts of other segments, make an effort to observe and recognize grammar in a similar manner.

Pay attention to the structures, patterns, and usage of grammar that are present in the texts. Try to identify and understand how different grammar points are employed within the context of the segment. By actively observing and analyzing the grammar used, you can enhance your understanding and application of Arabic grammar throughout your language learning journey.

STEP 9: LISTEN AGAIN

Make it a practice to revisit and listen to the segments you have previously studied at a later time. You will likely notice that your comprehension improves, and you can understand the content more easily compared to your initial attempts. This phenomenon can be attributed to the consolidation and organization of learned material that takes place in the brain during sleep, as studies have shown.

By revisiting the segments after a break or the following day, you reinforce your learning, solidify your understanding, and allow your brain to further process and integrate the acquired knowledge. This practice helps enhance your listening skills and overall retention of the Arabic language.

How do I study the dialect segments?

The dialect segments in the book present a valuable opportunity to study the various regional varieties of natural speech as spoken by native speakers. While each dialect has its unique characteristics, you will discover that they are not significantly different from one another. Despite differences in vocabulary, pronunciation, and grammar, you will come to realize that the majority of words in dialects are the same or very similar to those used in MSA.

Vocabulary: The Matching exercises in each dialect segment introduce words that are unique to the colloquial language of that specific dialect. However, you will observe that the majority of words overlap with MSA. The primary distinction lies in the most common words used in everyday language, such as pronouns, prepositions, demonstratives, conjunctions, adverbs, and commonly used verbs and nouns.

Pronunciation: As you study the text while listening, pay attention to vowel changes that differ from MSA. For example, in Egyptian Colloquial Arabic (ECA), "he writes" would be pronounced as يِكْتِب instead of the MSA pronunciation يَكْتُب. Additionally, listen carefully for the regional variations in the pronunciation of certain consonants, such as ظ, ط, ق, ذ, ج, ث, and ض, which may differ or be replaced by other sounds in certain dialects.

Grammar: The notes in the book highlight some of the more common and interesting grammatical idiosyncrasies the first time they appear in a segment. Keep an eye out for additional examples of these grammatical features in the text. Being aware of these differences in vocabulary, pronunciation, and grammar will greatly enhance your understanding of native speakers when conversing in their respective dialects.

Please note that LCA (Levantine Colloquial Arabic) refers to the continuum of dialects spoken in Syria, Lebanon, Palestine, Israel, and Jordan. Minor differences may be noticed between these dialects.

The Texts and Translations

Lines

The text and translation for each segment in the book have been divided into numbered "lines." These lines do not necessarily correspond to complete sentences or clauses but are instead manageable chunks of text that can be studied individually. This division allows for easier comprehension and analysis of the content within the text and translation. By breaking the text into these manageable lines, learners can focus on specific portions and explore the linguistic and grammatical features in a structured manner.

Voweling

A "minimalist approach" has been taken in voweling the Arabic text. That is, although the text contains *tashkeel,* the diacritic marks that show short vowels (ُ,ِ,َ), no vowel (ْ), and a double consonant (ّ), they are not written when predictable.

1. *Fatha* (َ) has been made the "default" vowel; as it is the most common vowel, it is normally not written in the texts. A consonant without a diacritic can be assumed to take fatha, except as noted below.
2. A final consonant is assumed to take *sukūn* (ْ) if unvoweled: سكن *sakan.* If it pronounced with a final vowel, this will be written: سكنَ *sakana.*
3. A consonant followed by a long vowel is unmarked: با *bā,* بي *bī,* بو *bū.* However, diphthongs are clearly marked: بَيْ *bay,* بَوْ *baw.* In dialects, these may represent ē and ō: بَيْ *bē,* بَوْ *bō.*
4. A final ية is assumed to be ـِيَّة.
5. The definite article ال is not marked with *sukūn* (ْ); however, when assimilated a *šadda* (ّ) is written above the following consonant: الشَّمس *aššams.* The vowel of the definite article is not written, although it may be pronounced ال in some dialects.
6. The prefixed word و *wa* in MSA, is pronounced in a variety of ways in dialects, such as *wi,* or *u.* Still, these are generally unmarked. Listen carefully to dialect segments to how the speaker pronounces this word.

Every attempt has been made to reflect the pronunciation used by the speaker in the tashkeel, regardless of whether the speaker has used the correct case suffix in MSA, or used voweling in a word considered non-standard.

Uh...

Fillers, which are used to indicate that the speaker is pausing or thinking about what to say next, are a common and natural part of spoken language. The pronunciation of fillers can vary among speakers and regions, but in order to make them easily recognizable, they have been transcribed as either الاه... or ممم... throughout the texts. Additionally, يَعني is a common filler in Arabic that can be translated as "that is" or "you know."

In spoken discourse, it is not uncommon for a speaker to make errors and then backtrack to correct themselves or rephrase a sentence. There may also be instances where a sentence is left unfinished. These occurrences are indicated by the use of ellipses (...) in the text, allowing you to identify that the word you may have missed is actually an incomplete word. The purpose of these ellipses is to assist you in deciphering the listening material. However, when you are reading for comprehension, anything preceding an ellipsis can be disregarded as it does not contribute to the overall meaning.

The Translations

In order to facilitate the matching of Arabic words and phrases with their translations, the emphasis has been placed on direct translations, sometimes at the expense of maintaining a stylistically pleasing rendition. However, you are encouraged to consider alternative ways in which lines could be translated into English. This approach allows for a more nuanced understanding of the text and promotes exploration of different translation possibilities. By engaging in this exercise, you can gain insights into the varied ways language can be expressed and expand your language skills beyond literal translations.

Notes

Notes follow the texts and are referenced within the text by the * and ⓘ symbols next to the line numbers. The asterisk (*) refers to a linguistic or cultural note, while ⓘ indicates an Internet link to a relevant article or video which you may find interesting. (The Wikipedia articles often contain links to an Arabic version that could provide further reading practice.)

ECA	Egyptian Colloquial Arabic	**MSA**	Modern Standard Arabic
ICA	Iraqi Colloquial Arabic	**TCA**	Tunisian Colloquial Arabic
LCA	Levantine Colloquial Arabic*	**YCA**	Yemeni Colloquial Arabic
MCA	Moroccan Colloquial Arabic		

Accompanying audio available at:

www.lingualism.com/audio

---

* including the Syrian, Lebanese, Palestinian, and Jordan dialects

Daily Routine

Key Words

مرْحلة (مراحِل) stage, phase, part   وحْش monster

Main Idea

a. Hend has a busy schedule and lots of responsibilities.
b. Hend has a lot of free time to pursue her hobbies.
c. Hend works far from home and only sees her family on weekends.
d. Hend feels lucky to have a lot of help from her family and housekeeper.

True or False

1. Hend's day consists of three parts.
2. Hend is **not** a morning person.
3. Hend usually drinks one cup of tea in the morning.
4. Hend's husband sometimes drives her to work.
5. Hend's son does his homework while she does housework.

Multiple Choice

1. Which two are true about Hend's son?

   a. He gets to school by bus.
   b. His father usually takes him to school.
   c. He is homeschooled by his grandmother.
   d. His grandmother watches him while Hend is at work.

2. Which meal does Hend **not** usually have at home?

   a. breakfast   c. dinner
   b. lunch   d. *none (She has all her meals at home.)*

3. What does Hend mention she does during her free time at work?

   a. She eats.   c. She helps students.
   b. She chats with colleagues.   d. *all of the above*

4. What time does Hend usually have dinner?

   a. 5 p.m.   c. 9 p.m.
   b. 7 p.m.   d. 11 p.m.

5. What does Hend call the last phase of her day?

   a. the mother's phase   c. the student's phase
   b. the housewife's phase   d. the teacher's phase

Matching

MSA	ECA	English
أَجْلِسُ	كُبَّاية	a little (bit)
أَحْضُرُ	شُوَّية	afterward
آخُذُ حَمَّامًا	علشان	and then
أرى	بِتاع	because; in order to
أُشاهِدُ	بعْدَ كِدا	cup
أَعْمَلُ	باتْفرّج على	free time
أنا مُتْعبة جِدًّا	باشوف	housewife
بعْدَ ذلِكَ (x2)	باشْتغل	I bring
ربّة بَيْت	جَوْزي	I don't have
زَوْجي	مِش	I see; I look at
عِبارة عن	شُغْل	I sit
عمل	أجيب	I take a shower.
قليلًا	وقْت فْري	I watch
كأْس	أقْعُد	I work
لِأَنَّ، لِكَيْ	بِيبْقى	I'm so tired.
لَيْسَ	سِتّ بَيْت	it is; he is
لَيْسَ عِنْدي	مِسْتنّي	my husband
مُنْتظِر	وبعْدَيْن	not
وقْت فراغ	أنا خلاص تِعِبْت	of
no translation	ما عنْديش	waiting
	آخذ شاوَر	work; job

Answers

Main Idea: a **True or False:** 1. F[2] 2. T[4] 3. F[14] 4. T[12] 5. F[32-33] **Multiple Choice:** 1. a[8] & d[26] 2. a[18] 3. d[18-21] 4. c[36] 5. c[39]
Matching: بعْدَ ذلِكَ afterward بعْدَ كِدا / of بِتاع / لِأَنَّ، لِكَيْ because; in order to علشان / قليلًا a little (bit) شُوَّية / كأْس cup كُبَّاية / شُغْل work; / لَيْسَ not مِش / زَوْجي my husband جَوْزي / أَعْمَلُ I work باشْتغل / أرى I see; I look at باشوف / أُشاهِدُ I watch باتْفرّج على / ربّة housewife سِتّ بَيْت / عِبارة عن it is; he is بِيبْقى / أَجْلِسُ I sit أقْعُد / وقْت فراغ free time وقْت فْري / أَحْضُرُ I bring أجيب / عمل job لَيْسَ عِنْدي I don't have ما عنْديش / أنا خلاص تِعِبْت I'm so tired. أنا مُتْعبة جِدًّا / بعْدَ ذلِكَ and then وبعْدَيْن / مُنْتظِر waiting مِسْتنّي / بَيْت آخُذُ حَمَّامًا I take a shower. آخذ شاوَر /

Text

يَوْمي بِيبْدأ السّاعة سِتّة الصُّبْح،	1*	My day starts at six o'clock in the morning,
وغالِبًا بِيتِقسّم لِأرْبع مراحِل:	2	and it is usually divided into four parts [phases].
أوّل مرْحلة وأصعْبها باسمّيها مرْحلة الوحْش،	3	I call the first phase, and the toughest one, the monster phase.
لِأنّي باكون في أسْوأ حالاتي على الإطْلاق أوّل ما باصْحى مِن النَّوْم.	4	This is because I'm usually in my worst mood as soon as I wake up.
بسّ بعْد أوّل كُبّاية شايْ باتْحسّن شُوّية.	5	However, after the first cup of tea I get a little better.
باصحّي ابْني وأفطّرُه،	6	I wake my son up and give him breakfast,
ااه... غالِبًا سنْدْوِتْش أوْ كَيْك وكُبّاية لبن.	7	uh... usually a sandwich or a cake and a glass of milk.
وبِلبّسُه وأنزّلُه علشان يِلْحق الباص بِتاع المدْرسة.	8*	I get him dressed and take him downstairs to catch the school bus.
بعْدَ كِدا بالْبِس أنا وأنا باتْفرّج على التِّليفِزْيُون.	9	Afterward, I get dressed while watching TV.
غالِبًا باشوف الأخْبار، وبانْزِل الشُّغْل حَوَالي السّاعة ثمانْية.	10	I usually watch the news, and I go to work around eight.
الجامْعة اللّي أنا باشْتِغل فيها بعيدة شُوّية،	11	The University where I work is a bit faraway,
ااه... فـ... لمّا جَوْزي بِيكون مَوْجود باطْلُب مِنُه إنُّه يِوصّلْني بالعربية.	12	uh... so, if my husband is around, I ask him to drive me there.
ااه... ولَوْ مِش مَوْجود باخُذ تاكْسي.	13	Uh... And if he's not around, I take a taxi.
أوّل ما باوْصَل الشُّغْل باشْرب كمان كُبّاية شايْ علشان أتْخلّص مِن أيّ أثر لِلوحْش بِتاع الصُّبْح.	14	When I arrive at work, I drink another cup of tea, in order to get rid of any traces of the morning monster.
ااه... وبابْدأ المرْحلة التانْية مِن اليَوْم وهِيّ مرْحلة الأسْتاذة.	15	Uh... And I start the second phase of the day: the teacher.
اممم... بابْدأ أدْخُل مُحاضراتي.	16	Um... I start giving my lectures.
الوقْت دا بِيعْدي بِسُرْعة جِدًّا، يِمْكِن علشان أنا بابْقى مُسْتمْتِعة به لِأقْصى درجة.	17	This time passes so quickly, probably because I enjoy it so much.
ااه... بَيْن المُحاضرات وبعْضها مُمْكِن أجيب فِطار مِن الكافْتيرْيا.	18	Uh... Between lectures, I get my breakfast from the cafeteria.
مُمْكِن أكون عامْلة سنْدْوِتْشات معايا...	19	Sometimes I have my own sandwiches.
ااه... و... ااا... الوقْت دا بِيكون ااه... وقْت فري مُمْكِن أقْعُد فيه أتْكلّم مَع زمايْلي في الشُّغْل،	20	Uh... and... uh... This time is uh... usually free time during which I can sit and chat with my colleagues.
أوْ مُمْكِن لَوْ فيه طالِب عنْدُه سُؤال بِيجيلي.	21	Or sometimes a student comes to me with a question.

ااه... لَوْ فيه مثلاً assignment هُوَّ عامْلُه وعايْزة أقولُّه comments عَلَيْه، امممم... بِيِبْقى هُوَّ الوَقْت دا المُناسِب.	22	Uh... If, for example, he has done an assignment and I want to give him comments on it, um... this time is usually the right time.
بَعْدَ يَوْمَ الشُّغْل ما بِيخْلَص ااه... باخُد ااه... مَيكروباص وبارْجع البَيْت.	23	After the work day ends, uh... I take uh... a microbus and go back home.
ااه... للأسف الجامْعة عنْدنا بعيدة شُوَيّة فما فيش تاكْسيات.	24	Unfortunately, our university is a bit far away, so there are no taxis.
وبتِنْتِهي المَرْحلة التانْية مِن اليَوْم كِده وتِبْدأ مرْحلة الأُمّ وسِتّ البَيْت.	25	The second phase of the day ends, and the phase of the mother and housewife begins.
ااه... اِنّي بِيْكون رجع مِن المَدْرسة ومِسْتنّيني عنْدَ جِدِّتُه (اللي هِيَّ حمّاتي).	26	Uh... [By then,] my son will have come from school and is waiting for me at his grandma's (my mother in law).
فباخُدُه وأروَّح البَيْت.	27	So, I take him and go home.
بِسُرْعة بِسُرْعة باجهِّز الغداء.	28	I quickly make lunch.
غالِبًا باكون مُحضَّراه مِن بالليْل بِحَيْث ما ياخُدْش مِنّي وقْت طَويل.	29	I usually have it prepared the night before, so that it won't take me long.
ااه... غالِبًا جَوْزي بِيْكون ااه... مِسافِر.	30	Uh... My husband is uh... away most of the time.
هُوَّ بِيِشْتغل على بُعْد أرْبع ساعات فبيْبات كْتير في الشُّغْل. فباتْغدّى أنا وابْني.	31	He works four hours away, so he often stays overnight at work, so I have lunch with my son.
بعْد الغدا باقْعُد معَ اِبْني ااه... أساعِدُه في المُذاكْرة وفي حلّ الواجِب.	32	Uh... After lunch, I sit with my son to help him study and do homework.
وبِعْدَيْن باسيبه هُوَّ يِتْفرَّج على التِّليفِزْيُون وبابْدأ أنا أرتِّب البَيْت.	33	Then I leave him watching TV and I start tidying up the house.
ااه... بَعْدَ ما بارتِّب البَيْت مُمْكِن أقْعُد أستريَّح شُوَيّة.	34	Uh... After I'm done tidying up the house, I rest for a little bit.
مُمْكِن أحْيانًا أخْطِفْلي نُصّ ساعة أتْفرَّج فيها على التِّليفِزْيُون وبِعْدَيْن أبْدأ في تجْهيز العشاء.	35	I might sneak in half an hour to watch TV, and then I start preparing dinner.
بِنِتْعشّى حَوالي السّاعة تِسْعة بالليْل.	36	We have dinner around nine p.m.
و ااه... بانيِّم اِبْني.	37	And uh... I put my son to bed.
وبِكِده تْخلَص المَرْحلة التالْتة بحمْد الله.	38	Thus ends the third phase! Thank God!
آخِر مرْحلة باقِة في اليَوْم هِيَّ مرْحلة الطالْبة.	39	The last phase of the day is the student's phase.
اِللي هِيَّ أنا المُفْروض أذاكِر فيها علشان الماجِسْتير طبْعًا.	40	This is when I'm supposed to study for my master's.

أنا باقول المفْروض لِأنّ في الغالِبِية العُظْمى مِن الأوْقات باكون أنا خَلاص تِعِبْت وما عنْديش أيّ اِسْتِعْداد إنّ أنا أركِّز في المُذاكْرة أوْ في أيّ حاجة	41	I say "supposed to" because most times I'm already too exhausted and not ready to concentrate on studying or on anything else.
فــ... غالِبًا بادْخُل آخُد شاوَر وأطْلع مِن الشاوَر، آخُد السّرير بالحِضْن وأنام لِحدّ تاني يَوْم.	42	So, I usually take a shower and give my bed a hug, and sleep till next day.

Notes

*1 Egypt Arabic, as many other dialects of Arabic, adds the prefix بِ bi- to mark the present tense.

*8 A common alternative to adding a possessive suffix directly to a noun is to add the definite article الـ to the noun and follow it by بِتاع with a possessive suffix: بَيْتي = البَيْت بِتاعي *my house.*

The Lebanese Identity

Key Words

هُويّة identity   حضارة civilization   أَصْل origin

Main Idea

Walid explains ___.

    a. the origin of the Lebanese identity
    b. how other Arabs see the Lebanese
    c. why the Lebanese are not really Arabs
    d. the impact of modern globalization on the Lebanese identity

True or False

1. Throughout history, many civilizations have invaded Lebanon.
2. The Phoenicians were the indigenous inhabitants of Lebanon.
3. Walid considers the Lebanese to be "non-Arabs".
4. Walid thinks the Lebanese culture is distinct from that of other Arab countries.
5. Switzerland once invaded Lebanon.

Multiple Choice

1. Lebanon's geographical location has made it ___ and ___.

    a. culturally diverse
    b. isolated from the Arab world
    c. a link between the East and West
    d. economically prosperous

2. Which civilization does Walid **not** mention as having invaded Lebanon?

    a. the Phoenicians
    b. the Arabs
    c. the Romans
    d. the Ottomans

3. Lebanon is known as "the Switzerland of the West" because of its people are ___.

    a. hospitable
    b. mercantile
    c. multilingual
    d. *all of the above*

4. Some people consider the Lebanese to be "non-Arabs" because ___.

    a. they are completely westernized
    b. they are not ethnically Arab
    c. they are often not Muslim
    d. they often cannot speak Arabic

5. The Lebanese differ from other Arabs because of ___.

    a. their economic prosperity
    b. their history of cultural diversity
    c. their bilingualism
    d. their Mediterranean coastline

Matching

بِشكْل أصحّ	according to
مُنْذُ القِدم	and others; etc.
بِفَضْلِ	but; however
وغَيْرِها	for this reason
لِهذا السّبب	more accurately
مِن هذا المُنْطلق	since antiquity
في يَوْمِنا هذا	thanks to
مِنْهُم من	that said; from that standpoint
وإنّما	there are those who...; some people...
بِحسبِ	these days

Answers

Main Idea: a **True or False:** 1. T[5] 2. F[16] 3. F[18] 4. T[19] 5. F[9-10] **Multiple Choice:** 1. a[3] & c[4] 2. b[6] 3. d[9-10] 4. b[12-15] 5. b[19-20]
Matching: بِشكْل أصحّ more accurately / مُنْذُ القِدم since antiquity / بِفَضْل thanks to / وغَيْرِها and others; etc. / لِهذا السّبب
for this reason / مِن هذا المُنْطلق that said; from that standpoint / في يَوْمِنا هذا these days / مِنْهُم من there are those
who...; some people... / وإنّما but; however / بِحسبِ according to

Text

صباح الخَيْر. المَوْضوع هُوَ الهُوِيّة اللُّبنانية	1	Good morning. The topic is the Lebanese identity,
وبِشكْل أصحّ ما هُوَ أصْل اللُّبنانيين.	2	and more accurately "What is the origin of the Lebanese?"
عرِفَ لُبنان مُنْذُ القِدم تنوُّع واسِع وشامِل في الحضارات.	3	Lebanon has known broad and comprehensive diversity in civilizations since ancient times.
فِبِفضْل مَوْقِعه الجُغْرافي على شَواطِئ البَحْر المُتَوَسِّط وكِصِلة وصْل بَيْنَ الشّرْق والغرْب،	4	Thanks to its geographical location on the shores of the Mediterranean and as a link between East and West,
أصْبحَ لُبْنان مُحطِّ أنْظار العَديد مِنَ الشُّعوب والحضارات القديمة الّتي قامت بِغزْوة والعَيْش فيه على مرِّ العُقود	5*	Lebanon has been the focus of attention for many peoples and ancient civilizations that have invaded and lived in it over the decades,
كالحضارة الفينيقية والبيزنْطية والرومانية والعُثْمانية وغَيْرِها.	6	such as the Phoenicians, the Byzantines, the Romans, the Ottomans, and others.
لِهذا السّبب أصْبحَ لُبنان غنيًّا بِتنوُّع حضاراتِه ولُغاتِه.	7	For this reason, Lebanon has become rich in the diversity of its civilizations and languages.

واكْتسَبَ اللُّبْناني مِن هذا المُنْطلق عِدّة هُويات فأصْبحَ قريبًا مِنَ الغرْب كقُرْبِهِ مِنَ العرب.	8	From this standpoint, the Lebanese have gained several identities, as it is close to the West and to the Arabs.
فعُرِفَ بالشّعْبِ المِضْياف، التّاجِر، المُتعدِّد اللُّغات.	9	It is known for its hospitable, mercantile, multilingual people.
لِذا أُطْلِقَ على لُبْنان لقب سُويسْرا الشّرْق.	10	Therefore, Lebanon has been given the nickname "the Switzerland of the East".
ففي يَوْمِنا هذا انْقسمت الأراء ووُجُهات النّظر حَوْلَ أصْل وتاريخ اللُّبْنانيون،	11*	Today, opinions and views about the origin and history of Lebanon are divided.
فمنْهُم من قال أنَّ اللُّبْناني هُوَ عربي ومِنهُم من قال أنَّ اللُّبْناني لَيْسَ عربيًا،	12	There are those who say that the Lebanese are Arabs, and there are those who say that the Lebanese are not Arabs,
وإنّما مِن عُروق غَيْر عربية يتكلّم العربية فقط لِمَوْقِعِه في البِلاد العربية.	13	but rather from non-Arab roots who speak Arabic only because of [Lebanon's] location among Arab countries.
بحسبِ التّاريخ والمَوْقِع فالنّظرية الثّانية لَيْست بحقيقة.	14	According to history and geography, the latter view is not factual.
فهُم يعْتِبرون أنّ أصْل اللُّبْنانيين فينيقي، أيّ لَيْسَ عربيًا.	15	They consider the origin of the Lebanese to be Phoenician, which is not Arab.
بَينما الفينيقيون لَيْسوا سُكّان لُبْنان الأصْليون	16	The Phoenicians were not the indigenous inhabitants of Lebanon,
إنّما عبروا بِه وأخذوهُ إلى حُكْمِهِم نظرًا لِقُوّتِه التِّجارية في القِدم.	17	but rather crossed over it and took it under their rule because of its trade strength in ancient times.
مِن هذا المُنْطلق يُمْكِنُنا القَوْل والجزْم أنّ اللُّبْناني هُوَ عربي	18	That said, we can decisively say that the Lebanese are Arabs,
وإنّما يتميّز عن غَيْرِه مِنَ العرب بِتعدُّد الحضارات والثّقافات	19	but they are distinct from other Arabs in their multiplicity of civilizations and cultures
التّي اتّخذتْهُ مَوْطِنًا لها فأغْنتْهُ بِصِفاتٍ عِدّة مَيّزتْهُ عن سائِر شُعوب العالم.	20	that took part in their formation and enriched them with several characteristics which, in turn, distinguished them among the people of all other nations of the world.

Notes

*5 Walid must have meant to say القُرون *centuries,* and not العُقود *decades.*

*11 As an idafa construction, the correct form should be تاريخ اللُّبْنانيّين, and not تاريخ اللُّبْنانيّون.

The Arabic Language

Key Words

نُطْق pronunciation	الفُصْحى Standard Arabic
لَهْجة dialect	اِخْتلِف، يخْتلِف to differ

Main Idea

a. Alaa compares her own dialect to Standard Arabic.

b. Alaa focuses on the modern uses for Standard Arabic, and briefly touches on regional dialects.

c. Alaa compares the Classical Arabic in used in the Quran to the Standard Arabic used today.

d. Alaa mentions dialects spoken in various regions, as well as touching on the uses of Standard Arabic.

True or False

1. The Maghrebi dialect contains a lot of Italian vocabulary.

2. Egyptian Arabic is the most popular and widely understood dialect.

3. The Egyptian dialect is fairly uniform throughout Egypt.

4. Children must learn Standard Arabic to read the Quran **and** pagan poetry.

5. The difference between the dialects and Modern Standard Arabic is minimal.

Multiple Choice

1. Alaa mentions that *qaf* ق is ___.

   a. a distinctive sound in Arabic   b. a difficult sound for English speakers

   a. not found in the Egyptian dialect   c. only used in some dialects

2. The Levantine dialects are spoken in Syria, Lebanon, ___.

   b. Jordan and Iraq   e. Palestine and Jordan

   d. Iraq and Kuwait   f. Palestine and Iraq

3. Which dialect contains the *ch* sound?

   a. the Libyan dialect   c. the Kuwaiti dialect

   b. the Egyptian dialect   d. *all of the above*

4. The Bedouins in Egypt speak a dialect similar to ___.

   a. the dialect of Cairo   c. the dialect of the Nubians

   b. the Gulf dialects   d. the Levantine dialects

5. Standard Arabic is used ___.

   a. in the news   c. for official government matters

   b. in historical dramas   d. *all of the above*

Matching

MSA	ECA	English
أرادَ (يُريدُ)	النِّهارْدة	a little (bit)
أشْياء	دِلْوقْتي	also; too
أنَّ	بِتاع	also; too
الآن	حاجات	and such; and the likes
أيْضًا (x2)	قَوِي	as; like
تُصْبِحُ	مِش	because; in order to; so that
جِدًّا	فيه	newspaper
جريدة	بِرْضُه	not
قليلًا	شِوَيَّة	not... at all
لِأنَّ، لِكَيْ	دي	now
لَيْسَ	زَيّ	of
لَيْسَ... إطْلاقًا	إنّ	other than that
ما عدا ذلِكَ	عايِز	she is; she becomes
مِثَلَ، كـ	كمان	that's all; that's it
هذِهِ، تِلْكَ	مِش... خالِص	that...
وما شابهَ ذلِكَ، إلخ	جُرْنان	there is; there are
وهذا كُلُّ ما في الأمْر	بِتِبْقى	things
يوجد، هُناكَ	عشان	this; that
اليَوْم	وكِدة	today
no translation	غَيْر كِدة	very
	بَسّ كِدة	want

Answers

Main Idea: d **True or False:** 1. F[17,19-20] 2. T[22-26] 3. F[27-29] 4. T[33,39] 5. F[38] **Multiple Choice:** 1. a[5] 2. c[12] 3. c[24-25] 4. b[31] 5. d[37] **Matching:** النِّهارْدة today اليَوْم / دِلْوقْتي now الآن / بِتاع of / حاجات things أشْياء / قَوِي very جِدًّا / مِش not لَيْسَ / فيه there is; there are هُناك يوجد، / بِرْضُه also; too أيْضًا / شِوَيَّة a little (bit) قليلًا / دي this; that هذِهِ، تِلْكَ / زَيّ as; like مِثَلَ، كـ / إنّ that... أنَّ / جُرْنان newspaper جريدة / بِتِبْقى she is; she becomes تُصْبِحُ / عايِز want أرادَ (يُريدُ) / كمان also; too أيْضًا / مِش... خالِص not... at all لَيْسَ... إطْلاقًا / غَيْر كِدة other than that ما عدا ذلِكَ / وكِدة and such; and the likes وما شابهَ ذلِكَ، إلخ / عشان because; in order to; so that لِأنَّ، لِكَيْ / تُصْبِحُ becomes / بَسّ كِدة that's all; that's it وهذا كُلُّ ما في الأمْر

Text

النِّهارْدة أنا حاتْكلِّم عن وضْع اللُّغة العربية دِلْوقْتي في العالم العربي.	1	Today I'm going to talk about the status of Arabic now in the Arab world.
ااه... في البِداية حابّة أقول إنّ اللُّغة العربية لُغة غنية جدًّا بالكلمات والمُصْطلحات و... بالأصْوات حتّى.	2	Uh... first, I'd like to say that Arabic is a very rich language in vocabulary and idioms and... even in sounds.
يعْني فيها أصْوات شامْلة مِن لُغات كِثير.. مثلًا فيها حرْف الخاء (خ) الـ... النُّطْق بِتاع الخاء، الغَيْن (غ)، الـ... ااه... العَيْن (ع)، الحاء (ح)،	3*	I mean it has sounds from many languages... for example it has the sound "kha", the... pronunciation of "kha", the "ghayn", the... uh... the "3ayn", the "Ha",
فـ... فيه حاجات كِثيرة قوي يعْني مِش... مِش مَوْجودة فـ... في لُغات تانْية، ااه... كحُروف ونُطْق.	4	so there are a lot of things that don't exist in other languages as letters and sounds.
ولكِن وفيه قاف (ق) برْضُه. ده... ده حرْف مُميَّز شوَيّة.	5	But there is also "qaf", and this is a bit of a distinctive letter.
ولكِن طبْعًا حاليًا اممم... اللُّغة العربية الفُصْحى بْتُسْتخدم بِشكْل رسْمي،	6	However, Modern Standard Arabic now is officially used,
ولكِن انْقسمت للهْجات كِثير قوي إحْنا بْنِتْكلمْها.	7	but has been divided into many dialects that we speak.
اممم... مِن اللهْجات الكِثير دي اللهْجة المِصْرية مثلًا.	8*	Um... among those many dialects is the Egyptian dialect, for example.
في مَصْر بِنتْكلِّم لهْجة مِصْرية تخْتلِف تمامًا عن العربية الفُصْحى.	9	In Egypt we speak an Egyptian dialect that is totally different from Standard Arabic.
الِّلي أنا بْتكلِّم بِها دي دِلْوَقْتي دي لهْجة مِصْرية، فيها كلِمات اممم... عربي وفيها كلِمات اممم... تُرْكي وفيها كلِمات قُبْطي.	10	The dialect I'm speaking right now is an Egyptian dialect. It has Arabic words, um... Turkish words, and it has Coptic words
وفيها كلِمات مِن الهيروغْليفية (المصْرية القديمة).	11	and it has words from Hieroglyphics (Ancient Egyptian).
في اللهْجة الشّامية، الِّلي بِيتْكلِّم بِها أهْل الشّام سَواء مِن سورْيا أوْ أُرْدُنّ أوْ فِلسْطين أوْ لُبْنان وكُلُّهُم تقْريبًا شبه بعْض.	12	In the Levantine dialect, which the people of the Levant speak, whether from Syria, Jordan, Palestine or Lebanon, all of them are almost the same.
باخْتِلاف... برْضُه في اخْتِلافات ما بَيْنَ اللهْجات نفْسها.	13	With a difference... But there are also differences between the dialects themselves.
ااه... السّوري مثلًا... يعْني مـ... بيِتْكلِّم بِـ... بِـ... بيِمْطّوا... الشّوام بيِمْطّوا في الكلام شوَيّة.	14	The Syrians for example, when they speak, they... stretch... the Levantines stretch the pronunciation a little bit.

مَثَلًا مِن ضَمْن الكَلِمات اللِّي أنا عارْفاها في السُّوري مَثَلًا إنَّ همّا ااه... بِيْقولوا مَثَلًا "بَلْكي".	15	For example, among the words that I know in Syrian is... they say "belki".
بَلْكي دي كِلْمة بَرْضُه تُرْكي يَعْني.	16*	Belki is also a Turkish word.
ااه... اللِّيبي مَثَلًا... اللَّهْجة اللِّيبي داخِل فيها كَلِمات إيطالي كَتير وده راجِع لِأنِّي... ااه... لِيبْيا كانِت مُحْتَلّة مِن إيطالْيا.	17	Uh... Libyan, for example... the Libyan dialect contains a lot of Italian vocabulary, and this is due to... uh... the fact that Libya was occupied by Italy.
مَثَلًا تَقْريبًا كُلّ أدَوات المَطْبَخ بِيسْتخدموها بالإيطالي.	18	For instance, almost all the kitchen tools they use are in Italian.
المَغْرب العربي بَرْضُه الـ. الـ. اللَّهْجة بتاعْتُه صَعْب جدًّا إنَّ إحْنا كمصرِيّين نفْهمْها.	19	Maghreb... Arabic also... its... its dialect is very difficult for us Egyptians to understand...
ااه... لِأن هِيَّ داخِل فيها لُغة فرنْسية كَتير،	20	uh... because it contains a lot of French vocabulary,
وده بَرْضُه راجِع لِأنَّ الجَزائِر وتونِس و... كانوا... كانوا تحت الاحْتِلال الفرنْسي في وقْت مِن الأوْقات.	21	and this is also due to the fact that Algeria and Tunisia and... were... were under French occupation at one time.
على عكْس اللَّهْجة المِصْرية... المِصْرية... اللَّهْجة المِصْرية مُمْكِن تِتْفهم مِن أيّ حد عربي.	22	This, unlike the Egyptian... Egyptian... Egyptian dialect, which can be understood by any Arab.
ااه... في الخليج مَثَلًا بَرْضُه لهْجتْهُم تخْتَلِف سَواء في السّعودية أوْ في الكُوَيْت ااه... أوْ في الـ... الـ... قطر والبحْرَيْن والإمارات...	23	Uh.... In the Arabian Gulf, for example, their dialect also differs, whether in Saudi Arabia or in Kuwait, uh... or in... Qatar, Bahrain, or the Emirates.
ااه... الكُوَيْت بالذّات لِهُم لهْجة غَريبة شُوَيَّة إنّهُم بِينْطقوا أيّ حاجة فيها حرف الكاف (ك) "تش" زَيّ الـ"ch" في الـ"English"،	24	Kuwait in particular has a bit of a strange dialect, as they pronounce anything ending in "kaf" as "ch" as "ch" in English.
فأنا لَوْ باقول مَثَلًا ااه... كِتابك... اللِّي هو مَعَ... يَعْني... كِتابك... حتِبْقى... بالمصْري... حتِبْقى بالـ... بالكُوَيْتي "كِتابْتش"... يَعْني... كِدة يَعْني. فدي نْتِبْقى بَرْضُه مُخْتلفة شُوَيَّة.	25	So if I say for example uh... "kitabak", which is... is ... in the Egyptian dialect, it would be in Kuwaiti "kibatach"... you know, like that. So it is also a bit strange.
ااه... زَيّ ما قُلْت إنَّ اللَّهْجة المِصْرية هِيَّ أسْهلُهُم وأكْترهُم ااه يَعْني... شَعْبية،	26	Uh... as I said, the Egyptian accent is the easiest and the most... uh... you know, popular,
حتّى إنَّ بعْض الـ... يَعْني كَتير مِن الأعْمال الفَنِّية اللِّي بِيْعْملْها ناس مِش مصرِيّين، بِيعْملوها باللُّغة المِصْرية.	27*	to the extent that some, I mean, a lot of the artistic works made by non-Egyptians, are made in the Egyptian dialect.

وعايزة أقول كمان إنَّ حتّى اللَّهْجة المصرية داخل فيها... يعْني بْتِخْتلِف مِن مكان لِمكان.	28	I also want to say that even the Egyptian dialect includes... I mean, differs from one place to another.
يعْني إحْنا في مصْر مثلاً في كلمات في القاهرة غَيْر... بِيبْقى لِها معْنى مُخْتلِف في إسْكنْدرية.	29	So in Egypt we have, for example, some words in Cairo... that has a different meaning in Alexandria.
غالِبًا بِرْضُه في لهْجة أهْل المدينة زَيّ القاهرة، إسْكنْدرية، الـ... الـ... الـ... المُدُن اللي هي... بـ... مُتميّزة بِالطّابِع الحضري عامّةً، بِيخْتلِفوا غَيْر مثلاً لهْجة النّوبة؛	30	For the most part, in the dialect of city people as in Cairo, Alexandria, the cities with... characterized as having an urban nature, they differ from, for example, the Nubian dialect,
دي مِش مفْهومة خالِص تُعْتبر لُغة لوْحْدَها، غَيْر لهْجة البّدو بِتِبْقى شبه العرب شِويّة... بِتِبْقى شبه الخليج... غَيْر اللهْجة الصعيدي... غَيْر لهْجة الفلاحين.	31	which is totally incomprehensible, and is considered a language itself... or the dialect of the Bedouins, which is somewhat like the dialect of the Arabs... like the Arab Gulf... or the dialect of Upper Egypt or the dialect in the countryside.
يعْني في الدَّوْلة لوحـْ... الدَّوْلة الواحْدة حنْلاقي اخْتِلاف في اللهْجات.	32	So in a single country, we will find differences in dialects.
اللُّغة العربية الفصْحى بقت بتُسْتخْدم... اااه... طبعًا يعْني... أغْلب... لازم نِتعلّمْها كُلّنا لأنّ بِنِقْرا بِها القُرآن، فهيَّ لُغة لِها قُدْسية.	33	Standard Arabic, is used, of course, I mean, most of... we all have to learn it, because we use it in reading the Quran, so it is a language of some sacredness.
وحتّى القُرآن يعْني مِش بِيتِقْرا بِاللُّغة العربية الفُصْحى زَيّ أيّ حاجة تانْية،	34	And even the Quran is not read like anything else in Standard Arabic,
مِش زَيّ الجِرْنان أوْ زَيّ الـ... الـ... اللُّغة العربية الرّسْمية، لأ، القُرآن بِيبْقى لِه حتّى قَواعِد مُعيّنة في التجْويد وكِدة... لِقِراءتُه...	35	not like newspapers, or like... official Arabic. No, the Quran has its own rules for recitation, so... to read it...
فيه بعْض الحُروف... يعْني عشان يطْلع بِنغمة مُعيّنة... عنْد.... لمّا نيجي بِنِرتّلُه يعْني؛ لمّا بِن... بِنْقوم بِترْتيل القُرآن.	36	there are some letters... so that it comes out in a certain tone... when we chant it... I mean, when we... chant the Quran.
اااه... عادة اللُّغة العربية الفُصْحى بِتُسْتخْدم في الـ... في الأخْبار، وفي المُسلْسلات التّاريخية، وفي الجهات الرّسْمية.	37*	Uh... usually Standard Arabic is used in... in the news, and in historical dramas (period pieces), and official authorities.
اااه... و... للأسف فيه فرْق شاسع ما بَيْنَها وما بَيْن اللهْجة... اللهْجات اللي إحْنا بِنسْتخْدمْها،	38	Ah... and unfortunately there is a huge difference between it and the dialect... dialects we use.
ولكِن المفْروض إنّ إحْنا مِن صُغرَنا بِنْتعلّم اللُّغة العربية الفُصْحى لِدرْجة إنّ إحْنا بِنِدْرِس الشّعْر	39*	However, we are supposed to have learned Standard Arabic from childhood, to the extent that we study Pagan poetry, which

الجاهِلي اِلْلي هُوَّ كان حتّى قَبْل عَصر ظُهور الإِسْلام، وفي كِثير مِنُه كلِمات ماتِت يعْني،		was even before the Islamic era, and there are many words that are no longer used,
ولكِن عشان نِدْرِس البَلاغة في العربي، وكِدة يعْني...	40	but [we learn it] in order to study the eloquence of Arabic and such.
وده هُوَّ وضْع اللُّغة العربية حالِيًّا؛	41	And that was the state of Arabic at the moment;
إِنّ هِيَّ بتُسْتخْدم في الجْهات الرّسْمية وفي القُرْآن طبْعًا وفي الـ... في الـ... في الشأْن الدّيني عامةً يعْني.	42	it is used by official authorities and in the Quran of course, and in... in ... religious matters in general.
غَيْر كِدة، بِنتْكلَّم كُلّ مكان حسب لهْجتُه.	43	Other than that, each region speaks its own dialect.
بَسّ كِدة.	44	That's it.

Notes

*3 A common alternative to adding a possessive suffix directly to a noun is to add the definite article الـ to the noun and follow it by بتاع with a possessive suffix: بَيْتي = البَيْت بِتاعي *my house*.

*8 Unlike MSA and most other dialects, the demonstrative particle follows the noun: البِنْت دي *this girl* (MSA: هذِهِ البِنْت).

*16 belki = *maybe*

*27 Here, *artistic works* refers to *movies* and *songs*.

*37 Tip: Regional dialects are spoken in soap operas and movies. If you want to practice listening to MSA dialogues, try watching *historical* dramas, such as *Omar,* available on YouTube with English subtitles (**bit.ly/1sQyrZl**).

*39 جاهِلي *Pagan* (lit. *ignorant*) refers to the pre-Islamic era.

Childhood Memory

Key Words

أَذْكُرُ I remember   مسْقط رأْس hometown

Main Idea

Lilia tells about ___.

- a.   her parents' divorce when she was a child
- b.   a family vacation to Slovakia
- c.   going to study in Canada
- d.   when her family moved abroad

True or False

1.   Lilia's parents decided to move to Slovakia for her education.
2.   Lilia was excited to move to Slovakia.
3.   Lilia was sent to a psychiatrist in Slovakia.
4.   Lilia moved back to Tunisia with her mother, while he father stayed in Slovakia.
5.   Lilia didn't see her father for four years.

Multiple Choice

1.   Lilia refers to ___ as her native country.

   a.   Slovakia   b.   Tunisia   c.   Canada   d.   *none of the above*

2.   Which of the following is **not** true?

   a.   Lilia didn't want to leave Tunisia.
   b.   Her family moved to Slovakia after she finished her first year of junior (preparatory) high school.
   c.   Lilia collapsed on the day they left; she had never accepted the idea of leaving.
   d.   Lilia was too sad to say good-bye to her friends in Tunisia.

3.   What kind of school did Lilia attend in Slovakia?

   a.   an American school   c.   a Slovakian school
   b.   a British school   d.   *She can't quite remember.*

4.   Which of the following **two** are true?

   a.   Lilia and her mother would visit her father in Slovakia during winter vacation.
   b.   Lilia and her mother would visit her father in Slovakia during summer vacation.
   c.   Lilia's father would visit Tunisia during winter vacation.
   d.   Lilia's father would visit Tunisia during summer vacation.

5. Lilia recently received a full scholarship to complete a doctorate in Canada, ___.

    a. and will be studying there for four years
    b. but has rejected it
    c. but will only go if her mother accompanies her
    d. and still cannot decide whether to go or not

Matching

مرّةً وأنا صغيرةٌ	actually
لِمُدّةِ أرْبع سنَوات	As for me, ...
عِنْدما	at that time
للغاية	for four years
أمّا بالنِّسبةِ لي، ...	no matter
سُرْعانَ ما	not for nothing
آنذاكَ	once when I was small
فِعْلا	soon
لِدرجةِ أنّ	to the point that...
في حينٍ	utterly; extremely
مهْما	when
لا لِشَيْء	while

Answers

Main Idea: d **True or False:** 1. F[2-3] 2. F[6,10,14] 3. T[29] 4. T[32] 5. F[33] **Multiple Choice:** 1. a[2] 2. d[15-19] 3. d[20-21] 4. a[33] & d 5. b[41-42] **Matching:** مرّةً وأنا صغيرةٌ once when I was small / لِمُدّةِ أرْبع سنَوات for four years / عِنْدما when / للغاية utterly; extremely / أمّا بالنِّسبةِ لي، ... As for me, ... / سُرْعانَ ما soon / آنذاكَ at that time / فِعْلا actually / لِدرجةِ أنّ to the point that... / في حينٍ while / مهْما no matter / لا لِشَيْء not for nothing

Text

أذْكُرُ مرّةً وأنا صغيرةٌ، عُمري آنذاكَ كانَ حَوالَيْ ااه... إثْنا عشرة سنةً،	1	I remember once when I was little, I was at the time about uh... twelve years old,
عِنْدما قرّرَ والدايَّ الانْتقالَ للعَيْش في سلوفاكيا، بلدي الأُمّ، وذلِكَ بِـ... سبب شُغْلِ والِدي.	2*	when my parents decided to move and live in Slovakia, my native country, because of my father's work.
ااه... فقد تلقّى عرْضًا مُغْريًا للعمل هُنالِكَ لِمُدّة أرْبع سنَوات.	3	Uh... he had received a lucrative offer for work there for four years.

أتذكّرُ حينها كُنْتُ في غُرْفتي ألْعبُ معَ صديقتي عِنْدما دخلت أُمّي لِتُعْلِنَ لي الخبر.	4	I remember I was in my room playing with my friend when my mother came in to tell me the news.
اااه... بِالنِّسْبةِ لها، كانَ الخبرُ اممم... سارًّا للغاية.	5	Uh... For her, the news was mmm... utterly delightful.
أمّا بِالنِّسْبةِ لي، هااا... كانَ... أَشْبهُ بِالصّدْمة!	6	As for me, huh... it was... more like a shock!
حتّى إنّي خِلْتُها تمْزحُ معي.	7	I even thought she was kidding me.
ولكِنْ سُرْعانَ ما تأكّدْتُ من صحّةِ الخبر	8*	Soon, however, I confirmed the authenticity of the news
عِنْدما سمعْتُ والدي يتحدّثُ إلى عمّتي في خُصوصِ هذا المَوْضوع.	9	when I heard my dad talking to my aunt regarding this subject.
هااا... كم كانَ مِنَ الصّعْبِ عليَّ مُواجهةُ الخبر!	10	Huh... How difficult it was for me to cope with the news!
لقد كُنْتُ شديدةَ التعلُّقِ بِأصْدِقائي، بِعائلتي، ااااه... بِمِدْرستي ومِدينتي، بِحارتي، بل وبِتونس بلدي!	11	I was quite attached to my friends, my family, uh... my school and my city, my neighborhood, indeed to Tunisia, my country!
ااااه... لم أكُنْ مُسْتعِّدةً أبدًا أنْ أُغادِرَ كُلَّ هذا وأرْحلَ بعيدًا، بعيدًا عن عائلتي وأصْدِقائي.	12	Ah... I was never prepared to leave all this and go far, far away from my relatives and friends.
أذْكُرُ كم بكَيْتُ تلْكَ اللَّيْلة، وكم حزِنْتُ.	13	I remember how much I cried that night and how sad I was.
كانَ الخبرُ أشْبهُ بِالكابوس.	14	The news was like a nightmare.
كُنْتُ آنذاكَ في نِهايةِ سنتي الأولى بِالمدْرسة الإعْدادية.	15	I was, at the time, at the end of my first year of junior high school.
فأتْممْتُ تلْكَ السّنة الدِّراسية ثُمَّ رحلْنا.	16	I finished that school year and then we left.
أذْكُرُ أنّي كُنْتُ مُنْهارةً يَوْمَ سفرنا.	17	I remember collapsing on the day we left.
لم أتقبّل أبدًا فِكْرةَ الرّحيل.	18	I had never accepted the idea of leaving.
ودعْتُ عائلتي وأصْدِقائي وفي داخلي حُزْنٌ عميق.	19	I bid farewell to my relatives and friends, with a deep sadness inside me.
وعِنْدما وصلْنا إلى بْراتيسْلافا، اممم... عاصمة سْلوفاكيا، كانَ والدايَّ قد رسّماني بِمِدْرسة أمْريكية ااااه... أوْ إنْجِليزية،	20	When we got to Bratislava, mmm... the capital of Slovakia, my parents enrolled me in an American... or British... school,
ههه... لا... لا أتذكّرُ تمامًا.	21	ha-ha... I don't... I don't remember exactly.
كُلُّ ما أسْتحْضِرُهُ هُوَ حُزْني الشّديد ورفْضي المُطْلق لِلذّهاب إلى المدْرسة.	22	All I can recall is my intense sorrow and my outright refusal to go to school.
فقد اشْتقْتُ كثيرًا إلى... إلى كُلِّ شَيْءٍ في وطني تونس. هذا رغْم أنّي كُنْتُ في مسْقط رأْسي!	23	I missed... everything a lot in my homeland, Tunisia, this despite the fact that I was in my hometown [i.e. birth place]!
فقد كُنْتُ أشْعُرُ بِالاسْتِياء والقلق المُتواصِل.	24	I was dismayed and continually anxious.
لم أكُنْ لِأقْبلَ الحَوارَ حتّى معَ والِدَيَّ.	25	I would not even talk with my parents.
هاالا... وفِعْلا مرِضْتُ نفْسيًّا.	26	Huh... and actually I wasn't mentally well.
ااااه... انْعزلْتُ على نفْسي.	27	Uh... I isolated myself.

ورفضْتُ الحديثِ معَ الجميع، رفضْتُ الاِنْدِماجَ في المدْرسة وأَصْبحْتُ أُعاني مِنَ الأرقِ كذلِك.	28	I refused to talk to anyone, refused to integrate into school, and I began to suffer from insomnia, as well.
أَذْكُرُ أَنّي تسبَّبْتُ في قلقٍ كبيرٍ لِأُمّي وأبي، لِدرجةِ أَنّهُما حاوَلا الاِسْتِعانة بِطبيبٍ نفْسيٍّ لِمُعالجتي.	29	I remember that I caused great concern to my mom and dad, to the point that they sought out a psychiatrist to treat me.
ولكِنّي لم أُبدِ أَيَّ تحسُّن، بل اِزْدادت حالتي سوءً.	30	But I did not show any improvement, but rather my condition worsened.
اااه... وكانتِ النّتيجة، هااا... كما توقَّعت، بل كما تمنَّيْت.	31	Uh... The outcome was huh... as expected, indeed as I had hoped.
وهيَ أَنّي عُدْتُ إلى تونس معَ والدتي، في حينَ واصلَ أبي عملهُ هُنالكَ لِمُدّة أَرْبع سَنَوات كاملة.	32	Namely, that I went back to Tunisia with my mother, while my father continued to work there for a full four years.
كُنّا نزورُهُ في عُطْلةِ الشّتاء، وكانَ يأْتي هُوَ خِلالَ العُطْلةِ الصّيْفية.	33	We would visit him during winter vacation, and he would come during summer vacation.
صحيحٌ كُنْتُ أَشْتاقُ إليْهِ كثيرًا،	34	True, I missed him very much,
ولكِنّي كُنْتُ واعية تمامَ الوعي أَنَّ ذلِكَ كانَ أَيْسَرَ عليَّ بِكثير مِن أَنْ أَرْحلَ أنا إلى سْلوفاكيا،	35	but I knew full well that that was much easier for me than me going to [live in] Slovakia
وأَقْضي أَرْبع سِنين مِن عُمري وأَتْرُكُ كُلَّ شَيْءٍ جميلٍ اِعْتدْتُ عليْهِ ورائي.	36	and spend four years of my life leaving everything beautiful I was used to behind me.
تِلْكَ التجْربة القاسية الّتي عِشتُها، وإنْ كانت مُؤَقّتة، فإنّها تركت في نفْسي وقْعًا كبيرًا.	37	That harsh experience that I went through, albeit temporary, left a significant impact on me.
والآن، أنا مُقْتنِعةٌ أَنّهُ لَيْسَ بِإمْكاني التّخلّي عن بلدي وعمّا اعْتدْتُ عليْهِ هُنا أَبدًا، ومهْما كلَّفني الأَمر.	38	Now, I am convinced that I cannot abandon my country and what I am used to here, ever, no matter what it may cost me.
فها قد مرّت أَكْثرُ مِن عشرةَ سِنينَ ولم أتغيّر.	39	More than ten years have passed, and I haven't changed.
فأنا إلى الآن غَيْرُ قادِرة على العَيْشِ في بلدٍ آخر غَيْرَ بلدي.	40	I am to this day unable to live in a country other than my own.
فقد تحصَّلْتُ مُأَخَّرًا على مِنْحةٍ كاملةٍ لِلدِّراسة في كندا... لِأَرْبع سَنَوات لِأَسْتكْمِلَ مرْحلةَ الدُّكتوراه هُنالك.	41	I recently received a full scholarship to study in Canada... for four years, to complete a doctorate there.
ولكِنّي بِكُلِّ بساطة رفضْتُها، لا لِشَيْء ولكِنّي فقط لا أَسْتطيعُ الإِبْتِعاد عن أحبّتي!	42	But I simply rejected it, not for nothing, but I just cannot stay away from my loved ones!

Notes

*2 A little background information on Lilia: Lilia's father is Tunisian, and her mother is Slovak. Lilia was born in Bratislava, but her family moved to Tunisia when she was two or three years old. The term بلدي الأُمّ actually means *my native country* (lit. *my motherland*), and **not** *my mother's country.*

*8 Lilia says صَحّة *ṣaḥḥaᵗ* instead of the commonly accepted MSA pronunciation صِحّة *ṣiḥḥaᵗ*. This is a good example of how native speakers sometimes carry over regional pronunciations of certain words from their dialects into MSA. This is often because they're unaware that these are regionalisms.

Arabs in Israel

Key Words

الیَهود Jews   جَیْش army; military   gap فجْوة

Main Idea

The situation for Arabs in Israel ___.

- a. is far from perfect, but it is improving over time
- b. is increasingly becoming more unbearable
- c. is tantamount to slavery
- d. is idyllic these days, although it was horrendous in the past

True or False

1. Jews make up the majority of the population in Wasem's village.
2. Wasem sees an advantage of being a minority.
3. Arab villages are continually developing.
4. There is a large gap between the Jewish majority and minorities such as Arabs **and** Russians.
5. Wasem asks you, the listeners, not to prejudge an entire people.

Multiple Choice

1. Which of the following is **not** true?

    - a. Arabs in Israel receive I.D. cards from the state.
    - b. Arabs in Israel are not recognized as Israeli citizens.
    - c. Arabs do not serve in the Israeli army.
    - d. The standard of living among Arabs in Israel is quite low.

2. Arab communities do not get much funding from the Israeli government because ___.

    - a. they are funded by neighboring countries
    - b. Arabs do not serve in the military
    - c. Arabs are not citizens
    - d. *none of the above*

3. An advantage of being a minority that Wasem mentions is that members of a minority ___.

    - a. stick together and help each other
    - b. do not have to serve in the military
    - c. receive special government benefits
    - d. *none of the above*

4. Many people fear Arabs in Israel because ___.

    - a. they may be terrorists
    - b. they will soon be the majority
    - c. they're associated with drugs and crime
    - d. of the language barrier

5. Which of the following is **not** true?

    a. In the past, Arabs could only work in simple jobs, such as agriculture.

    b. Nowadays, you may find Arabs working in places such as Jewish laboratories.

    c. Even nowadays discrimination prevents many Arabs from working in Jewish factories and shops.

    d. Nowadays, Arabs can serve in the Israeli military.

Matching

MSA	LCA	English
أبي	بدّي	also
أخي	كمان	but
أُريدُ	عايْلة	family
إلَيْكَ	مناخُذ	he works
أوَدُّ أنْ	كْثير	I want
أيْضًا	هاي الـ	I'd like to...
جِدًّا	اِللي	is still
جعلَ	خلّا	it has caused
الّذي، الّتي	بِعْملوا	my brother
سنَوات	أبوْي	my father
عائلة	بِشْتغل	that; which; who
ما زال	بسّ	there is; there are
ناخُذُ	فيه	they do
هذِهِ الـ	أخوْي	this ___
ولكِن	سنين	to you
يعْملُ	لِسّة بعْدُه	very
يفْعلونَ	أنا حابِب	we get
يوجدُ	إلاك	years

Answers

Main Idea: a **True or False:** 1. F[4] 2. T[18] 3. T[13] 4. F[26] 5. T[40] **Multiple Choice:** 1. b[6-10] 2. b[9-10] 3. a[18] 4. c[23-24] 5. d[10]
Matching: اِللي / هذِهِ الـ this هاي الـ / جِدًّا very كْثير / ناخُذُ we get مناخُذ / عائلة family عايْلة / أيْضًا also كمان / أُريدُ I want بدّي / يعْملُ he works بِشْتغل / أبي my father أبوْي / يفْعلونَ they do بِعْملوا / جعلَ it has caused خلّا / الّذي، الّتي that; which; who بسّ / أنا حابِب I'd like لِسّة بعْدُه / ما زال is still سنين / أخي / أخوْي my brother سنَوات / years / يوجدُ / فيه there is; there are ولكِن / but أوَدُّ أنْ to you إلَيْكَ / إلاك to...

Text

مَرْحَبًا. أنا اليَوْم بِدّي حدِّثْكُم عن حَياة العربي في إسْرائيل.	1	Hello. Today I want to talk with you about the life of Arabs in Israel.
أنا أصْلي عربي مِن هذي البِلاد وكمان كُلّ العايْلة.	2	I am a native Arab from this country, and so all my family.
قريتْنا قرْية جتّ عُمْرها أكْثر مِن مِيّة سنة.	3	Our village is the village of Jatt, which is more than a hundred years old.
قريتْنا كُلّ سُكّانْها عرب.	4	The entire population of our village is Arab.
مِناخُذ الخِدْمات مِن شركات إسْرائيلية على اعْتِبار إنّه البلد مَوْجودة في دَوْلة إسْرائيل.	5*	We get services from Israel companies considering that the town is on Israeli land.
كُلّ العرب في إسْرائيل باخْذوا هُويات إسْرائيلية مِن الدَّوْلة.	6	All Arabs in Israel receive I.D. cards from the state.
وحسب قَوانين الدَّوْلة، العرب مِثْلْهُم مِثْل كُلّ السُّكّان في الدَّوْلة.	7	According to the laws of the state, Arabs are like any other citizen in the country.
مُسْتَوى الحَياة عِنْد العرب في إسْرائيل واطي كْثير	8	[However,] the standard of living among Arabs in Israel is very low
بِسبب قِلّة التَّمْويل مِن الدَّوْلة	9	because of the lack of funding from the government
بِحِجّة إنّه العرب ما بِخْدِموش في الجَيْش.	10*	on the grounds that Arabs don't serve in the army.
فما بِطْلَعْلهُمْش مصاريف مِثْل ما بِطْلَع لِلخادِم في الجَيْش.	11	So they don't get funds like those who serve in the army do.
كْثير مِن النّاس بِعْتِبْروا الشَّيْء كعُنْف ضِدّ العرب	12	A lot of people consider this as violence against Arabs,
ولكِنْ ما تزال القُرى والمُدُن العربية تِتْطوّر وتِكْبر مع الوقْت.	13	but Arab villages and cities are still evolving and growing over time.
العرب في هاي الدَّوْلة هُمْ القِلّة	14	The Arabs in this country are a minority,
والبشر في طبيعتهُم لمّا بِحِسّوا إنّهُم قِلّة قليلة بِبْداوْا يِتْكانْفوا مع بعْض.	15	and when humans, by their very nature, feel they are in a small minority, they stick together.
فمثلًا لمّا يِمْرض عربي ويروح على المُسْتشْفى	16	For example, when an Arab gets sick and goes to the hospital,
العايْلة كُلْها بِتيجي معْه وبِتظَلّ معْه لِحدّ ما يِتْحسّن.	17	the whole family comes with him and stays with him until he is well.
هاي واحِدة مِن الحسنات إنّك تِكون مع الأقّلية	18	This is one of the good things about being in a minority
لِأَنّ مِنْساعِد بعْض، مهْما كان الثَّمن.	19	because we help each other at any price,
وهذا الشَّيْء عكْس باقي الدُّوَل اِللّي فيها أكْثَرية عربية،	20	unlike other countries where Arabs are the majority,

فيها العربي ما بِيهْتمّ كْثير للعربي الثّاني.	21	where Arabs don't care about other Arabs.
وضْع الاقْتِصاد للعرب في إسْرائيل مُتدنيّ.	22	The economic situation for Arabs in Israel is low.
هذا الشَّيْء سبّب وُقوع الكِثير مِن العرب في عالم المُخدّرات والحرام.	23	This has caused many Arabs to fall into the world of drugs and crime.
وُقوع العربي في هذا النَّوْع مِن المشاكِل خلّا اليَهود والسَّاكْنين الآخرين في الدَّوْلة يخافوا مِن العرب.	24	Arabs being mixed up in such things has caused Jews and other residents in the country to fear Arabs.
فقليلْهُم العرب اِلّي بصحِّلْهُم يِشْتغلوا في مصانع أوْ محلات لليَهود في الدَّوْلة.	25	Therefore, few Arabs get the chance to work in Jewish factories and shops in the country.
هذا الشَّيْء أدّى للأسف لتكْبير الفجْوة بَيْن العرب والسُّكّان الآخرين في الدَّوْلة مِن اليَهود أوْ الرّوس أوْ أيّ عِرْق ثاني.	26	This has unfortunately led to an increase in the gap between Arabs and other citizens in the country, be they Jews or Russians or other ethnic groups.
هذي الفجْوة أدّت لتقْليل مُسْتَوى التّطوُّر عِنْد العرب،	27	This gap has led to a lower level of development for Arabs.
فظلّ مُعْظم العرب يعْملوا اليَوْم في الزِّراعة أوْ أعْمال مِهنية بسيطة مِثْل أبوّي،	28	So most Arabs today still work in agriculture or in simple jobs, like my dad;
بِشْتغل ميكانيكي.	29	he works as a mechanic.
و... بسّ كُلّ هذا كان مِن الماضي، فاليَوْم أصْبح فيه باحْثين عرب بِشْتغلوا في مُخْتبرات بِمْتلِكْها اليَهود،	30	But this is all in the past, for there are now Arabs who work as researchers in laboratories that belong to Jews,
مِثْل أخوّي الكِبير بِشْتغل في مجال هنْدسة الآلات الطِّبّية أكْثر مِن ثلاث سنين.	31	like my older brother, who has been working in biomedical research for over three years now,
وأنا باتْعلّم تمْريض وباشْتغل في مُسْتشْفى كقوّة مُساعدة.	32	and me studying nursing and working as an orderly in a hospital.
لِسّة بعْدُه وضْع العرب في إسْرائيل واطي والكراهية ضِدّ العرب مَوْجودة،	33	The status of Arabs in Israel is still low and hatred against Arabs exists,
ولكِن ومعَ الزّمن الكراهية بِتخْتفي	34	but with time it is disappearing,
والوضْع بِتْحسّن أكْثر.	35	and the situation is becoming better and better.
اتْفكّروش إنّه قضية العرب في الدَّوْلة هِيّ قضيهة نادْرة.	36	Don't think that situation for Arabs in [this] country is rare;
بالعكْس، هاي القضية مَوْجودة تقْريبًا في كُلّ العالم،	37	on the contrary, this case has been found almost everywhere in the world,

مِثل اِسْتِعْباد اليَهود في مصْر القَديمة على زمن الفراعنة	38	like the enslavement of Jews in ancient Egypt during Pharaonic times,
لِحدّ تِجارة العَبيد في الوِلايات المتّحِدة الأمْريكية.	39	and even the slave trade in the United States of America.
أنا حابِب أسْتغِلّ الفُرْصة وأطْلُب مِن كُلّ واحِد سامِعْني إنّه يِفكّر أكْثر مِن مرّة قبْل ما يِحْكُم على شعْب كامِل.	40	I would like to take this opportunity and ask everyone listening to me to think twice before judging an entire people,
لأنّه مُمْكِن هذا الشّعْب هُوَّ الصّديق الوحيد إلاك.	41	because this people may be your only friend.
شُكْرًا جزيلًا على اِسْتِماعْكُم.	42	Thank you for listening.

Notes

*5 Levantine Arabic, as many other dialects of Arabic, adds the prefix ‍ـبـ b- to mark the present tense. However, the 1st person plural adds ‍ـمـ instead.

*10 The negative is formed by sandwiching a verb (or particle) with ما...ش.

Daily Routine

Key Words

روتين routine   قُوّة مُساعِدة orderly; assistant   تعْليم learning; classes

Main Idea

Wasem has a busy daily routine.

    a.   First, he goes to school. Then he goes to his job.
    b.   First, he goes to his job. Then he goes to school.
    c.   He studies from morning until late in the evening.
    d.   He works from morning until late in the evening.

True or False

1.   Wasem prays first thing in the morning.
2.   Wasem starts work at eight o'clock in the morning.
3.   Wasem works at Loewenstein hospital.
4.   Wasem relaxes in his car until his shift starts.
5.   Wasem has two days off a week.

Multiple Choice

1.   Wasem is ___ years old.

    a. nineteen   b. twenty   c. twenty-one   d. twenty-two

2.   Wasem leaves home early in order to ___.

    a. study in the library   c. avoid traffic
    b. have breakfast at school   d. go to the mosque for the morning prayer

3.   Every day Wasem has ___.

    a. four 60-minute classes with 30-minute breaks between them
    b. three 90-minute classes with 15-minute breaks between them
    c. two two-hour classes with a one-hour break between them
    d. *none of the above*

4.   At the hospital, Wasem helps patients who are ___.

    a. amputees   c. visually impaired
    b. suffering from cancer   d. mentally ill

5.   Before Wasem goes to bed, he ___ and ___.

    a. makes himself dinner   c. watches TV
    b. studies   d. prays

Matching

MSA	LCA	English
أَذْهَبُ إلى	بِدّي	but
أُريدُ	باروح على	cup; glass
إزْدِحام مرور	بدْري	early
أَصِلُ	عشان	half
أَعْمَلُ	كِثير	hand
أُنْهي	أزْمات السِّير	I arrive
جِدًّا	باوْصِل	I finish
الّذي، الّتي	كاسة	I go to
رِجْل	أصْحابي في التّعْليم	I want
زملائي في الدِّراسة	اللي	I work
قدح	نُصّ	in order to; so that...
لكِن	باخلّص	leg; foot
لِكَيْ	بسّ	school friends
مُبَكِّرًا	فيه	there is; there are
نِصْف	إجْر	traffic (jams)
يَد	إيد	very
يوجدُ	باشْتغل	which; who; that

Answers

Main Idea: a **True or False:** 1. T⁵ 2. F¹³,²¹ 3. T¹⁷⁻¹⁸ 4. F²¹ 5. T³⁶⁻³⁷ **Multiple Choice:** 1. c² 2. c⁹ 3. b¹³⁻¹⁵ 4. a²³

5. a³² & d³⁴ **Matching:** بِدّي I want أُريدُ / باروح على I go to أَذْهَبُ إلى / بدْري early مُبَكِّرًا / عشان in order to; so that... كِثير / لِكَيْ /
very جِدًّا / أزْمات السِّير traffic (jams) إزْدِحام مرور / باوْصِل I arrive أَصِلُ / كاسة cup; glass قدح / أصْحابي في التّعْليم school friends زملائي
في الدِّراسة / اللي which; who; that الّذي، الّتي / نُصّ half نِصْف / باخلّص I finish أُنْهي / بسّ but لكِن / فيه
there is; there are يوجدُ / إجْر leg; foot رِجْل / إيد hand يَد / باشْتغل I work أَعْمَلُ

Text

مرْحبا. أنا اليَوْم بِدّي أحدِّثُكُم عن روتين حَياتي اليَوْمية.	1	Hello. Today I want to talk about my daily routine.
أنا شابّ اِبْن واحِد وعِشْرين سنة.	2	I'm a twenty-one-year-old guy.
باتْعلّم تمْريض وباشْتغل في مُسْتشفى كقُوّة مُساعِدة.	3*	I'm studying nursing and I work in a hospital as an orderly.
أنا باصْحى من النَوْم في السّاعة خمْس ونص الصُّبْح.	4	I wake up at five thirty in the morning.
باتْوضّى وباصلّي صلّاة الصُّبْح.	5	I perform ablution and the morning prayer.

بانْزِل على المطْبخ في نفس الوقْت إمّي بِتْكون تِجهِّز في الفُطور.	6	I go down to the kitchen at the same time my mother's preparing breakfast.
بأكُل فُطوري وباطْلع مِن الدّار السّاعة سِتّة بِسَيّارْتي الشّخْصية وباروح على مُسْتشْفى مأْئير.	7	I eat my breakfast and leave the house at six o'clock by car and go to the Meir hospital.
في هذا المُسْتشْفى باتْعلّم تمْريض.	8	At this hospital, I'm studying nursing.
أنا باحِبّ أطْلع بدْري مِن البيْت عشان أتْجنّب كُلّ أزْمات السّير في الطّريق،	9	I like to leave home early to avoid all the traffic on the roads.
مع أنّي باوْصل بدْري كِثير بسّ على الأقلّ باوفّر بنْزين لمّا أطْلع قبل كُلّ أزمات السّير.	10	Even though I arrive early, at least I save gas if I set out before all the traffic.
باوْصل حَوالي السّاعة سبْعة وباشْرب كاسة شاي أوْ قهْوة قبل كُلّ شيْء.	11	I arrive around seven o'clock and have a cup of tea or coffee before all else.
وباجْلِس معَ أصْحابي في التّعْليم، خُصوصًا أصْحاب الِّي بِطْلعوا بدْري مِن بُيوتْهُم مِثلي.	12	And I sit with my school friends, especially friends who leave their homes early like me.
في السّاعة ثماني بابْدأ التّعْليم الِّي هُوَ عِبارة عن ثلاث مُحاضرات.	13	At eight o'clock, I start my lessons, which consist of three classes.
كُلّ مُحاضرة ساعة ونُصّ مِن مَواضيع مُخْتلِفة مُتعلِّقة بالتّمْريض	14	Each class is an hour and a half on various topics related to nursing,
وبيْن كُلّ مُحاضرة خمسْطاشر دقيقة اسْتِراحة.	15	and between each class is a fifteen-minute break.
في السّاعة وحدة باخلّص التّعْليم.	16	At one o'clock I finish studying.
بعْد التّعْليم بارْكب بِسَيّارْتي وباروح على مُسْتشْفى ثاني اسْمُه لفينْشْطين.	17	After my classes, I get in my car and go to another hospital called Loewenstein.
أنا باشْتغل في هذا المُسْتشْفى.	18	I work in this hospital.
دَوامي بِبْدأ مِن السّاعة ثلاث بسّ أنا باوْصل بادْري حَوالي السّاعة وحدة ورُبْع.	19	My shift starts at three o'clock, but I arrive early at about a quarter past one.
في هذا المُسْتشْفى غُرْفة لِلأكْل معَ دفْع مُسْبق، يعْني بادْفع وبادْخُل لِلأكْل.	20	In this hospital, the cafeteria is pre-paid, that is, I pay and go in to eat.
بعْد الأكْل باجْلِس أرْتاح في حديقْة المُسْتشْفى لِحدَّ ما بِبْدأ الدّوام في السّاعة ثلاث.	21	After eating, I sit relaxing in the hospital's garden until my shift starts at three.
لمّا بِبْدأ الدّوام باطْلع لِقِسْم العظام وإعادة التّاهيل.	22	When my shift starts, I go up to the orthopedics and rehabilitation department.
في هذا القِسْم فيه مرْضة سُكّري أوْ مُصابين مِن حَوادِث طُرُق أوْ عمل، وانْقطع إجْر أوْ إيد.	23	In this ward, there are diabetics and those who have been injured in traffic or work accidents and have had feet [legs] or hands amputated.
بيجوا عنّا عشان بِتْعلِّموا كيف بِعيشوا معَ العاقِتْهُم.	24	They come to us to learn how to live with their disabilities.
أنا باشْتغل كقُوّة مُساعدة.	25	I work as an orderly.

باساعِد المَرْضة على العُبور مِن السَّرير لِلكُرْسي المُتحرِّك	26	I help patients from their beds to their wheelchairs,
وباساعِدْهُم في التَّنقُّل في القِسْم.	27	and I help them to get around the ward.
في السَّاعة خمْس ونُصّ مِنْجهِّز العشاء ومِنْدخِّل المرْضة عشان ياكُلوا.	28	At five thirty, we prepare dinner and bring the patients in to eat.
بعْد العشاء مِنْساعِد كُلّ مريض يِرْجع على السَّرير ومِنْجهِّزْهُم لِلنَّوْم.	29	After dinner, we help each patient back to his bed, and we get them ready for sleep.
بخْلُص دَوامي حَوالي السَّاعة أحْداش.	30	I finish my shift at about eleven o'clock.
باوْصِل البَيْت في السَّاعة أحْداش وخمْس وأرْبعين دقيقة.	31	I get home at eleven forty-five.
بادْخُل البَيْت وباجهِّز لِنفْسي عشاء بسيط.	32	I go in the house and make myself a simple dinner.
بعْد الأكل باصلّي صَلاة العشاء	33	After eating, I perform the evening prayer,
وأروح أنام في حَوالي السَّاعة اِطْناش ونُصّ بِاللَّيل.	34	and I go to bed around twelve thirty at night.
حَياتي مُرْهِقة نَوْعًا ما بسّ أنا مِتْعوِّد علَيْها.	35	My life is tiring, more or less, but I'm used to it.
هذا هُوَ الرّوتين حَياتي اليَوْمي، ما عدا يَوْمَيْ الجُمْعة والسّبْت طبْعًا	36	This is my daily routine, except for on Fridays and Saturdays, of course,
لِأنّهُم يَوْمَيْ راحة علَيّ.	37	because they're my days off.
شُكْرًا جزيلًا على اِسْتِماعْكُم.	38	Thank you very much for listening.

Notes

*3 Levantine Arabic, as many other dialects of Arabic, adds the prefix بـ b- to mark the present tense.

Marriage

Key Words

زَواج marriage	شابّ young man
خُطْبة engagement	فتاة young woman

Main Idea

Razanne talks about ___ and ___.

- a. the divorce rate in Syria
- b. wedding traditions in Syria and around the Arab World
- c. various kinds of engagement in cities and the countryside, in the past and in the present
- d. the average ages when people get married

True or False

1. Most men get married between the ages of twenty-five and thirty-five.
2. Girls in the countryside usually get married in their teens.
3. Traditionally, parents are involved in finding a potential spouse for their son or daughter.
4. Razanne uses 'loving relationships' as a euphemism for 'illicit relationships'.
5. Razanne says that Islam encourages marriage at an early age.

Multiple Choice

1. Most city girls wait until they ___ to get married.

   - a. have at least finished high school
   - b. are in their thirties
   - c. are pregnant
   - d. have started their careers

2. Razanne herself got married ___ college.

   - a. before   b. during   c. after   d. *She doesn't say.*

3. The traditional, or arranged, marriage ___.

   - a. is quite rare nowadays
   - b. is only found in villages
   - c. is becoming less common nowadays
   - d. is illegal in modern-day Syria

4. In a non-traditional engagement, a young man and woman might ___.

   - a. live together before getting married
   - b. elope
   - c. meet through their families
   - d. meet at work or school

5. Razanne believes that, in Syrian society, 'illicit relationships' are ___.

   - a. non-existent   b. uncommon   c. very common   d. *She doesn't say.*

Matching

تتراوَح ما بَيْنَ... إلى...	and then
تقْريبًا	approximately; about
بِالنِّسْبة لِـ	as for; when it comes to
لَيْسَ لها علاقة في	at least
أيْ	for a long time
على الأقلّ	it is still, to this day,...
هِيَ ما زالت إلى الآن	mostly; usually
مُنْذُ زمن	over time
ومِن ثُمَّ	range between ... and ...
معَ مُرور الوقْت	since; because
غالِبًا	that is (to say); i.e.
إلى حدّ ما	there must be
لا بُدّ مِن	they have nothing to do with
بِما أنَّ	to some extent

Answers

Main Idea: c & d **True or False:** 1. T[2] 2. T[8] 3. T[17-18] 4. F[24] 5. T[29] **Multiple Choice:** 1. a[11] 2. d 3. c[21] 4. b[22] 5. b[25-27]

Matching: تتراوَح ما بَيْنَ... إلى... / range between ... and ... / تقْريبًا approximately; about / بِالنِّسْبة لِـ as for; when it comes to / لَيْسَ لها علاقة في they have nothing to do with / أيْ that is (to say); i.e. / على الأقلّ at least / هِيَ ما زالت إلى الآن it is still, to this day,... / مُنْذُ زمن for a long time / ومِن ثُمَّ and then / معَ مُرور الوقْت over time / غالِبًا mostly; usually / إلى حدّ ما to some extent / لا بُدّ مِن there must be / بِما أنَّ since; because

Text

الآن سأتحّدث عن الزّواج في العالم العربي عامّةً وفي سوريا ودِمشق خاصّةً.	1	Now I will talk about marriage in the Arab world in general and specifically in Syria and Damascus.
اممم... أعْمار الرّاغِبين في الزّواج تقْريبًا للشّباب تتراوَح ما بَين خمْسَ وعِشْرين سنة إلى اِثْنان وثلاثون تقْريبًا.	2*	Um... The ages of guys wishing to marry range from twenty-five to thirty-five approximately.

3	طَبْعًا هَذِهِ... هَذا لَيْسَ رقْم دقيق ولَكِن أنا اممم... أنا أضَع هَذِهِ النِّسْبَة بِناءً على خِبْرَتي وبِناءً على الأشْخاص الّذين أعرفُهُم والّذين تزوَّجوا في هَذا العُمْر تَقْريبًا.	Of course this is... this is not an exact figure, but I um... I put this figure based on my experience and based on the people I know, who have gotten married around this age.
4	بالنِّسْبَة لِلبنات تتراوَح الاااه... أعْمارُ الزَّواج ضِمْنَ فِئَتَيْن:	For girls, the age uh... to get married varies within two categories:
5	أوَّل فِئة عُمرية هِيَ... تَقْريبًا هِيَ تتركَّز الاااه... عِنْدَ الأرْياف أوْ على أطْراف المُدُن.	the first age group... more or less focuses on uh... rural areas or the outskirts of cities.
6	اممم... وهِيَ في المَناطِق الّتي تتْبعُ العادات والتّقاليد القديمَة والّتي لَيْسَ لها علاقة في... بِدين أوْ بِأيّ شَيْء.	Um... And these in areas that follow old customs and traditions, which have nothing to do with religion or anything.
7	يـ... هِيَ فقط تقاليد مُجْتمعية.	They are just community traditions
8	اممم... تَقْريبًا أعْمار هَذِهِ الفِئة تتراوَح بَيْنَ خمْسة عشر إلى تسْعة عشر سنة لِلفَتَيات.	Um... Roughly, the ages in this group range from fifteen to nineteen years for girls.
9	الاااه... أمَّا بالنِّسْبَة لِلفِئة الثّانية وهيَ فِئة الفَتَيات الّذين نشأْنَ... اللّاتي نشأْنَ في المُدُن مثلًا داخِل دمشق.	Uh... As for the second category, which is the category of girls who grow up... who were raised in cities, for example, in Damascus.
10	الاااه... نِسْبة الأعْمار الاااه... تَقْريبًا تتراوَح بَيْن عِشْرين سنة إلى سبْع وعِشْرين سنة أوْ سِتّة وعِشْرين سنة،	Uh... the ages uh... range approximately between twenty years old and twenty-seven, or twenty-six,
11	أيْ اممم... على الأقَلّ على الفتاة أنْ تكون قد أنْهت المَرْحلة الثّانَوية أوْ تقوم بالدّراسة الجامعية	that is, um... the girl has at least completed secondary school or is studying at university,
12	وهُناك بَعْض الفَتَيات الاااه... يُفَضِّلْنَ أنْ يُنْهينَ المَرْحلة الدّراسية الجامعية قبْلَ أنْ يتزوَّجْن.	and there are some girls prefer to their university education before they marry.
13	الاااه... بالنِّسْبَة لي شخْصيًّا، مُعْظم الاااه... صديقاتي الاااه... انْتظرْنَ حتّى أنْهينَ المَرْحلة الجامعية ثُمَّ الاااه... قُمْنَ بالزَّواج.	Uh... For me personally, most of uh... my friends uh... waited until they had finished university, and then uh... got married.
14	طَبْعًا هُناك نَوْعَيْن مِنَ الاااه... الـ... الخُطْبة في المُجْتمع السوري	Of course, there are two types of uh... engagement in Syrian society.
15	الاااه... أوَّل نَوْع وهُوَ النَّوْع التّقْليدي وهِيَ الخُطْبة التّقْليدية.	Uh... the first type, which is the traditional type, is the traditional engagement.
16	هِيَ هَذِهِ الخُطْبة الّتي الاااه... كانت الاااه... دارجة مُنْذُ اممم... مُنْذُ زمن، مُنْذُ مئة أوْ مِئَتَيْن سنة أوْ أقْدم	It is this engagement uh... the... which has been prevalent for ages, for a hundred or two hundred years or longer,
17	وهِيَ ما زالت إلى الآن الخُطْبة التّقْليدية وهِيَ أنْ يقوم الـ... أهْل الشّاب بالتّعرُّف على أهْل الفتاة	and it's still the traditional engagement today, whereby the young man's family becomes acquainted with the young woman's family,
18	ومِن ثُمَّ بَعْد أنْ يحْصُل هُناك تطابُق مِنَ النّاحِية الاِجْتِماعية والمادّية والثّقافية، الاااه... يعـ... يقوم أهْل	and then after they've seen eye to eye on social, material, and cultural points, the uh... the young man's family will put forward the

الشّابّ بـ... اااه... طرْح فِكرة خُطْبة اااه... الـ... هذِهِ الفتاة المُعيّنة على الشّابّ على ابْنِهِم.		idea uh... of an engagement with this suitable young woman to their son.
اااه... فَيقوم هذا الشّابّ بِالتّعرُّف على هذِهِ الفتاة طبْعًا ضِمْنَ جَوّ عائِلي معَ أُسْرتِهِم.	19	Uh... and the young man will get to know the young woman in a family atmosphere, with their families.
اااه... ومِن ثُمَّ اااه... يتقدّم لِخُطْبتِها و اااه... ومِن ثُمَّ الزّواج.	20	Uh... and then uh... will propose to her, and uh... then get married.
أمّا بِالنّسْبة للنّوْع الثّاني مِنَ الخِطْبة فهِيَ الخُطْبة الغَيْر تقْليدية. اااه... وهِيَ الآن اااه... مُنْتشِرة وتنْتشِر أكْثر معَ مُرور الوقْت.	21	The second type of engagement is the non-traditional engagement, uh... which is now, uh... widespread and spreading further with the passage of time.
اممم... وهِيَ أنْ اااه... يقوم الشّابّ والفتاة بِالتّعرُّف على بعْضِهِم. اااه... مُمْكِن أنْ يكون هذا الشّيْء في الجامِعة أوْ في العمل أوْ في الطّريق... أيّ مكان، أوْ عن طريق أصْدِقاء.	22	Hmm... The young man and woman meet each other, uh... possibly at university or at work or on the street... anywhere or through friends.
بعْدَ التّعرُّف بيْنهُم اااه... تكون اااه... الخُطْبة ناتِجة عن علاقة حُبّ بيْنَ الشّابّ والفتاة.	23	After they get to know each other, uh... uh... getting engaged is a result of a loving relationship between the young man and woman.
طبْعًا لا أقْصِد بِعلاقة الحُبّ أيّ شيْء مِثل اااه... الـ... علاقات الغَيْر شرْعية،	24	Of course, I do not mean by 'loving relationship' anything like uh... illicit relations.
غالِبًا العلاقات الّتي... المُنْتشِرة في المُجْتمع السّوري هِيَ علاقات حُبّ، تقْريبًا مُمْكِن أنْ نقول إنّها بريئة إلى حدّ ما.	25	Most relationships which are common in Syrian society are loving relationships, which we can more or less say are innocent to some extent.
لا... لا يدْخُل موْضوع العلاقة الجسدية بيْنَ... في هذا اااه... في هذا التّصْنيف.	26	The relationship does not... does not fall into the category of a physical relationship between...
لا بُدّ مِن أخْطاء فرْدية ولكِن هِيَ ليْستِ الحالة السّائِدة في المُجْتمع.	27	There must be individual transgressions, but this is not the situation prevailing in society.
اااه... لأنَّ الدّينَ الإسْلاميّ... بِما أنّي أنا مُسْلِمة فأنا أتحدّث مِن وُجْهة نظر المُسْلِمين...	28	Uh... because the Islamic religion... since I am a Muslim, I am talking from the perspective of Muslims.
الدّين الإسْلاميّ طبْعًا يحُثّ على الزّواج بِعُمْر مُبكّر وذلِكَ لِإنْشاء أُسْرة صالِحة، ترْبية أوْلاد و اااه... أيْضًا لِإعْفاف النّفْس عن أيّ علاقات غَيْر شرْعية.	29	Islam, of course encourages marriage at an early age in order to create a stable family, raise children, and uh... also to remain chaste from any illicit relations.
فإذًا اممم... هذا بِالنّسْبة لِأنْواع الخُطْبة لديْنا. شُكْرًا.	30	So, uh... those are the types of engagements we have. Thank you.

Notes

*2 Here, اِثْنَان وثلاثون should actually be اِثْنَيْن وثلاثين. The grammar involved in numbers in MSA is complex and undoubtedly poses a challenge for every learner. It may be comforting to know that even Arabs, whose dialects have comparatively simplified grammar, often have trouble with numbers in MSA, most notably the correct usage of ـون and ـين. In Arabic dialects, 20, 30, 40, etc. always end in ـين. MSA, however, requires that these numbers take ـون in the nominative case. More often, the mistake that Arabs will make is to use ـين, as they would in their dialects, when ـون is required. Here, however, we see a case of *hypercorrection,* whereby Razanne is aware that اِثْنان وثلاثون are MSA words, but she ends up using them when اِثْنَيْن وثلاثين would have actually been correct.

The Curse of the Pharaohs

Key Words

لعْنة curse   (فراعنة) فِرْعَون pharaoh   مقْبرة tomb

Main Idea

a. King Tutankhamun's tomb is cursed.

b. Legends of the Curse of the Pharaohs have been around since ancient times.

c. Strange phenomena surrounding the Curse of the Pharaohs have been scientifically documented.

d. There are several stories about the Curse of the Pharaohs, but these are not based in science.

True or False

1. The term Curse of the Pharaohs appeared after the discovery of the tomb of Tutankhamun.

2. Lord Carnarvon was trampled to death by a horse.

3. All legends of the Curse of the Pharaohs are connected to the tomb of Tutankhamun.

4. Fungi has been found inside some tombs.

5. Hieroglyphic symbols were first decoded in the early twentieth century.

Multiple Choice

1. The tomb of Tutankhamun was discovered by ___.

    a. Lord Carnarvon   c. Howard Carter
    b. King Ahmose I   d. a little boy

2. A ___ got into Howard Carter's house and killed his pet.

    a. cobra   c. mosquito
    b. hawk   d. scorpion

3. It is said that large number of workers present during the opening of the tomb of Tutankhamun ___.

    a. believed that a hawk circling overhead was the god Horus
    b. died due to a mysterious fever
    c. were unexplainably able to read the hieroglyphics on the tomb's walls
    d. *all of the above*

4. After a young boy stared into the eyes of a mummy, ___ and ___.

    a. he was cured of his illness
    b. he died due to a mysterious illness
    c. he could read hieroglyphics
    d. was able to lead archeologists to the location of the tomb of Tutankhamun

5. Scientists attribute the deaths that followed the opening of the tomb of Tutankhamun to ___.

    a. gases and poisonous fungi found inside the tomb
    b. malaria from mosquitos infesting the tombs
    c. the Curse of the Pharaohs
    d. pure coincidence

Matching

في بِدايات القرْن العشْرين	a large number of
وذلِك بِسبب	able to
في الحقيقة	afterward
ثُمّ	and this led to…
عِنْدما	because of
وأدّى ذلِك إلى	consequently
بدلًا مِنَ	during
عِبارة عن	earlier
عددًا كبيرًا مِنَ الـ	in fact
أثْناء	in the early the 20th century
وبعْدَها	in the late 19th century
سابِقًا	instead of
لم… بعْد	is; are
ما يعْني أنَّ	not… yet
في نِهايات القرْن التّاسِع عشْر	then
وبِالتّالي	when
قادِر على	which means

Answers

Main Idea: d **True or False:** 1. T[1-2] 2. F[12] 3. F[20] 4. T[28] 5. F[34] **Multiple Choice:** 1. c[13] 2. a[13-15] 3. b[19] 4. a[23] & c[24] 5. a[27-28] **Matching:** في بدايات القرْن العشْرين / in the early the 20th century / وذلك بِسبب because of / في الحقيقة in fact / ثُمَّ then / عددًا كبيرًا مِنَ الـ a large number of / أثْناء during (أثْناء) / عِبارة عن is; are / بدلًا مِنَ instead of / وأدَّى ذلِك إلى and this led to... / عِنْدما when / في نهايات القرْن التّاسِع عشر in the late 19th century / ما يعْني أنَّ which means / لم... not... yet / بعْد earlier / سابِقًا afterward / وبعْدَها during / قادِر على able to / وبِالتّالي consequently

Text

ظهرَ مُصْطلح "لعْنة الفراعِنة" في بِدايات القرْن العشْرين	**1**	The term "Curse of the Pharaohs" appeared at the beginning of the twentieth century,
وخاصّة بعْدَ اكْتِشاف مقْبرة الملك توت عنْخ آمون،	**2**	especially after the discovery of the tomb of King Tutankhamun,
وذلِك بِسبب حُدوث مجْموعة مِنَ الحَوَادِث الغريبة والغامِضة الّتي تلت اكْتِشاف تِلْك المقْبرة.	**3**	due to the occurrence of a series of strange and mysterious incidents that followed the discovery of that tomb.
في الحقيقة لا يوجد أيّ تعْريف أوْ ذكر عِلْمي لِهذا المُصْطلح في الأبْحاث،	**4**	In fact, there is no scientific definition or mention of this term in research,
ولكِن تمَّ إطْلاقُه على الحَوَادِث الغريبة والغامِضة الّتي تحْدُث بعْد اكْتِشاف المومياوات أوِ التّعامُل معها.	**5**	but it was unleashed with the strange and mysterious incidents that occurred after the discovery or handling of the mummies.
أمّا عن تِلْك الحَوَادِث الّتي أكّدت من أُسْطورة لعْنة الفراعِنة فهِيَ حالات الوفاة الّتي تبِعت فتْح مقْبرة الملك توت عنْخ آمون،	**6**	As for those incidents which confirmed the legend of the curse of the Pharaohs are the deaths that followed the opening of the tomb of King Tutankhamun,
وأهمّها وفاة اللّورد كارْنافون الّذي كان يُموِّل بعْثة اسْتِكْشاف المقْبرة،	**7**	most notably the death of Lord Carnarvon, who had funded the mission to search for the tomb,
والّذي حدث أنّه بعْد اكْتِشاف المقْبرة لدغت اللّورد كارْنافون بعوضة.	**8**	and who happened to have been bitten by a mosquito after the discovery of the tomb.
ثُمَّ جُرِح هُوَ في مكان اللدْغة عِنْدما كان يحْلِق ذقْنَه،	**9**	Then he was wounded where he was stung while he was shaving his beard,
مِمّا تُسبِّب في إصابته بِتسمُّم في الدّم، وأدَّى ذلِك إلى إصابته بِحُمّى شديدة أدَّت إلى وفاته.	**10**	which caused blood poisoning, and this led to a high fever which led to his death.
وبعْد ذلِك مات والدُه حُزْنًا علَيْه،	**11**	And after that, his father died from grief over him,
وأثْناء تشْييع جنازته دهس الحِصان الّذي كان يحْمِل النعْش طِفْلًا صغيرًا وقتله .	**12**	and during his funeral, the horse carrying the casket trampled a little boy, killing him.
أمّا الحادِثة الّتي حدثت معَ هَوَارْد كارْتر مُكْتشِف المقْبرة هِيَ أنّه كان يحْتفِظ بِعُصْفور كناريا في قفصٍ في منْزِله	**13**	The incident which occurred with Howard Carter, the discoverer of the tomb, is that he kept a canary in a cage in his house

ويَوْم تَمَّ كَسْر قُفْل المَقْبرة تسلَّلت أفْعى مِن نَوْع الكوبْرا وهُوَ نَوْع الأفْعى الَّذي كانَ يَحْمي مَقْبرة المِلك، والتهمت هذِه الأفْعى عُصفور الكَناريا،	14	and the day that the tomb's lock was broken on the tomb, a cobra, which is the kind of snake that protected the tomb of the king, sneaked in and devoured the canary,
وعِنْدما عادَ هَوَارْد كارْتر وجد أنَّ الأفْعى جالِسة في القفص بدَلًا مِنَ العُصفور.	15	and when Howard Carter returned, he found the snake sitting in the cage instead of the bird.
ويُقال أَيْضًا أنْ عِنْدَ كَسْر خَتْم المَقْبرة لوحِظَ أنَّ هُناك صقْرًا يُحلِّق فَوْقَ المَقْبرة.	16	It is also said that when the tomb's seal was broken, it was observed that there was a hawk circling over the tomb.
والصقْر كانَ مِنَ الطُّيورِ المُقدَّسة عِنْدَ الفراعِنة	17	The Falcon was a sacred bird of the pharaohs,
وكان يُعْتقد أنَّ الإله حورُس الَّذي يتجسَّد في جسِد المَلِك عِبارة عن صقْر.	18	and it was believed that the god Horus, who is embodied in the body of the king, is a hawk.
ويُقال أَيْضًا أنّ عددًا كبيرًا مِنَ العُمّال الَّذين كانوا مُتَواجِدين أثناء فتْح المَقْبرة قد تُوفّوا بِسبب حُمّى غامِضة.	19	It is also said that a large number of workers who were present during the opening of the tomb died due to a mysterious fever.
ولم ترْتبِط أساطير لعْنة الفراعِنة بِمَقْبرة توت عنْخ آمون فقط، ولكِن تردَّدت الكثير مِنَ الخُرافات والحِكايات حَوْلَ تِلْكَ اللعْنة.	20	Legends of the curse of the pharaohs are not only connected to the tomb of Tutankhamun, but a lot of myths and tales about that curse have been circulated.
وكانَ أكْثرُها جذْبًا لِلإنتِباه هِيَ حادِثة تتعلَّق بِصبي كان مريضًا وكانَ يُحِبُّ مِصْرَ القديمة.	21	The most striking is an incident involving a boy who was sick and who loved ancient Egypt.
ثُمَّ حدث ذاتَ يَوْم أنْ ذهب هذا الصّبي إلى المَتْحف المِصْري.	22	Then it happened one day that this lad went to the Egyptian Museum.
وكانَ يُحدِّق بِشدّة في عَيْنَي مومِياء المَلِك أحْمُس الأوّل، ثُمَّ حدثت مُعْجِزة شفت هذا الصّبي	23	He was staring deeply into the eyes of the mummy of King Ahmose I, when a miracle occurred that cured this boy.
وبعْدَها أصبح هذا الفتى قادِرًا على قِراءة كُلِّ شَيْء يجِدُهُ في الآثار المِصْرية القديمة، خاصَّةً الآثار المُرْتبِطة بِفتْرة الهُكْسوس،	24	Afterward, the boy was able to read everything he found in ancient Egyptian ruins, especially the ruins associated with the Hyksos period.
والأساطير الَّتي تتحدَّث عن لعْنة الفراعِنة لا تُعدُّ ولا تُحْصى.	25	Legends about the curse of the Pharaohs are countless.
ولكِن كما ذكرْنا سابِقًا لا يوجد أيّ أثْبات عِلْمي لِتِلْكَ اللعْنة.	26	But as we mentioned earlier, there is no scientific proof of that curse.
أمّا التفْسير العِلْمي الَّذي صاحِب تِلْكَ الظّاهِرة هُوَ انْحِباس الغازات في داخِل المَقْبرة بِسبب غلْقِها لآلاف السّنَوات،	27	The scientific explanation that accompanies this phenomenon is the entrapment of gases inside the tomb because of it being closed for thousands of years.
ووُجِدت في بعْض المَقابِر آثار لِفُطرِيات.	28	And traces of fungi have been found in some tombs.

لَمْ يُثْبَت بَعْد ما إذا كان القُدماء هُم مَن يَزْرعون تِلْكَ الفُطْرِيات بِهدف حِماية المَقْبرة	29	It has yet to be proven whether it was the ancients who would plant these fungi in order to protect the tombs
أوْ إذا كانَ غَلْق المَقْبرة لِفترات طَويلة هُوَ ما يُكوِّن تِلْكَ الفُطْرِيات.	30	or if it was that the tombs being closed for long periods of time that produced fungi.
أمّا سبب ارْتباط تِلْكَ اللّعنة بِمقْبرة توت عنْخ آمون على وجْه الخُصوص فلهُ عِدّة أسْباب،	31	As for the link of that curse to the tomb of Tutankhamun in particular, there are several reasons for it.
أهمُّها أنّ مقْبرة توت عنْخ آمون لَمْ تُمَسّ أبَدًا قبْلَ أنْ يَسْتكْشِفها هَوَارْد كارْتر،	32	most notably that Tutankhamun's tomb had remained untouched before it was discovered by Howard Carter,
ما يَعْني أنّها كانت مُغْلَقة لِأكْثر مِن ثلاثة آلاف عام.	33	which means they had been closed for more than three thousand years.
والسّببُ الثّاني هُوَ أنّهُ لَمْ تكُن رُموز الهيروغْليفية قد تمّ تفْسيرها قبْل نِهايات القرْن التّاسع عشَر،	34	The second reason is that hieroglyphic symbols had not been decoded until the late nineteenth century
وبِالتّالي لَمْ يكُن أحد قادِرًا على قِراءة التّعاويذ المكْتوبة على جُدْران المقابِر	35	and thus no one was able to read the incantations written on the walls of the tombs.
وهِيَ العِبارات الّتي تسبّبَت في بثّ الرُّعْب في قُلوب مُسْتكْشِفي المقابر،	36	These phrases caused the spread terror in the hearts of the tomb explorers,
مِثْلَ التّعْويذة الّتي كانت مكْتوبة على جُدْران مقْبرة توت عنْخ آمون	37	such as the spell written on the walls of the tomb of Tutankhamun
والّتي تقول "سيَذبح المَوْت بِجناحَيْه كُلّ من يُحاوِل أنْ يُبدِّد أمْن وسلام مرْقِد الفراعِنة."	38	which says "Death slaughters, with its wings, whoever tries to disturb the peace of the pharaoh's resting place."

Focus

أمّا __ (ف)...   as for __, ...

This structure introduces a new topic. Alaa uses it four times in this segment. Copy these occurrences and their translations into the table below.

أمّا __ (ف)...	English

Traffic Accidents

Key Words

حَوادِث سَيْر traffic accidents   مُعْضِلة dilemma
سائِق driver   حلّ (حُلول) solution

Main Idea

a. There are several reasons behind the high number of traffic fatalities in Morocco.
b. The rate of traffic accidents in Morocco has increased drastically in recent years.
c. The rate of traffic accidents in Morocco has decreased in recent years.
d. The Moroccan government is to blame for the situation.

True or False

1. Traffic accidents account for 13% of all deaths in Morocco.
2. Illiteracy is one cause of traffic accidents in Morocco.
3. Abdelhak mentions that traffic accidents are a burden on the state treasury.
4. One problem is that the government has **not** introduced punishments for traffic violations.
5. In Morocco, you can have your driver's license revoked for traffic violations.

Multiple Choice

1. The annual number of traffic fatalities is approximately ___.

   a. 400   c. 4,000
   b. 1,400   d. 14,000

2. ___ is the main cause of traffic accidents.

   a. Poor road conditions   c. Drinking and driving
   b. Drag racing   d. Speeding

3. ___ respect traffic lights.

   a. Drivers do not   c. Pedestrians do not
   b. Pedestrians   d. Neither drivers nor pedestrians

4. Which is **not** explicitly mentioned as a problem?

   a. driving without a license   c. not respecting the right of way
   b. drinking and driving   d. poor road conditions

5. What does Abdelhak think needs to be done?

   a. a national debate   c. educating people
   b. studying the problem   d. *all of the above*

Matching

أَعْتَقِدُ أَنَّ	And let's not forget…
المُعَدّل	for example,
فعلى سبيل المِثال،	however; but rather
هذا دونَ أَنْ نَنْسى	I think; I believe that…
مِن أَجْلِ	in my opinion
بِما في ذالِكَ	in order to; for
في نظري	including
وإنّما	must
يجِب	rate; average
عن طريق	through; via

Answers

Main Idea: a **True or False:** 1. F[4] 2. T[9] 3. T[11] 4. F[13-14] 5. T[14] **Multiple Choice:** 1. c[3] 2. d[7] 3. d[9] 4. a[8,10] 5. d[16-17]

Matching: أَعْتَقِدُ أَنَّ I think; I believe that… / المُعَدّل rate; average / فعلى سبيل المِثال، for example, / هذا دونَ أَنْ نَنْسى And let's not forget… / مِن أَجْلِ in order to; for / بِما في ذالِكَ including / في نظري in my opinion / وإنّما however; but rather / يجِب must / عن طريق through; via

Text

يُعْتبرُ المغْرب واحِدًا مِن الدُّوَل الّتي تعْرِفُ نِسب حَوادِث سَيْر كثيرة.	1	Morocco is a country with very high rates of traffic accidents.
أَعْتَقِدُ أَنّهُ لا يكادُ يَمُرُّ يَوْم دونَ أَنْ تُطْلِعَنا وسائِل الإعْلام والجرائِد عن وُجودِ حَوادِث سَيْر مُميتة بِمُخْتَلف مُدُن المغْرب.	2	I think hardly a day passes without us hearing in the media and newspapers about there being fatal traffic accidents in various cities of Morocco.
أَظُنُّ أَنّهُ لا يقِلُّ المُعَدّل السنَوِي عن أَرْبعة آلاف قتيل سنَوِيًّا،	3	I think it's at least an annual rate of four thousand deaths a year,
وتقْريبًا حَوالي ثلاثة في المِائة مِن نِسبة الوَفَيات بالمغْرب.	4	approximately… about three per cent of the deaths in Morocco.
هذا المُعَدّل مُخيفٌ جِدًّا.	5	This rate is very scary.
ويُرْجِع الخُبراء هذِه الحَوادِث إلى أَسْباب مُتعدِّدة ومُتنَوِّعة.	6	Experts attribute these incidents to numerous and various causes.
فعلى سبيل المِثال، تَحْتَلُّ السُّرعة المُفْرِطة المرْتبة الأُولى في أَسْباب حَوادِث السَيْر	7	For example, excessive speed occupies first place in the causes of traffic accidents,

بِالإِضافة إلى السّيا... سِياقة التّهَوُّر وعدم اِحْترام الأَسْبَقية والتّجاوُز المعيب والحالة الميكانيكية السيئة للعربات،	8	in addition to reckless dri... driving and not respecting the right of way, passing cars improperly, and poor mechanical conditions of the vehicles,
وعدم اِنْتِباه الرّاجِلين والأُمِّية وعدم إلمام السّائِقين بِقَوانِ... بِقانون السَّيْر وعدم اِحْترام كُلّ مِن الرّاجِلين والسّائِقين للإِشارات الضَّوْئية وعدم اِحْترام علامة قِف.	9	the lack of attention to pedestrians, illiteracy, drivers not knowing laws, and both drivers and pedestrians not respecting traffic lights and stop signs.
هذا دونَ أَنْ نَنْسى الحالة السَّيئة لِأَغْلب الطُّرُق بالمَغْرِب بِالإِضافة إلى عدم الوَعْي وشُرْب الخمر أثناء السِّياقة.	10	And let's not forget the poor state of most roads in Morocco, in addition to inattention and drinking alcohol while driving.
كُلّ هذا جعلَ المَغْرِب يُفكِّر في إيجاد حُلول لِهذِهِ المُعْضِلة الّتي تُكلّف خزينة الدَّوْلة كثيرًا.	11	All this had made Morocco think about finding solutions to this dilemma, which is quite a burden on the state treasury.
فكانَ الحلّ هُوَ إخْراج مُدَوّنة للسَّيْر تقوم بِسَن... بِسَنِّ عُقوباتٍ زجرية في حَقّ المُخالِفين؟	12	Is the solution is to put out a traffic code to enact deterrent punishments against violators?
كما اتّخذت الحُكومة المَغْربية مجموعة مِن الإِجْراءات مِن أجْل الحَدّ مِن كثْرة حَوادِث السَّيْر	13	The Moroccan government has also taken a series of actions in order to reduce traffic accidents,
بِما في ذالِكَ العقوبات الحبْسية والغرامات المالية الثقيلة وسحْب رُخص القيادة.	14	including prison sentences, heavy fines, and revoking drivers' licenses.
في نظري اااه... إنّ مُعْضِلة حَوادِث السَّيْر لا يُمْكِن الحَدّ مِنْها بَيْنَ عشية وضُحاها	15	In my opinion, the dilemma of traffic accidents cannot be reduced overnight,
وإنّما يجب القيام بِمُناظرة وطنية مِن أجْل دِراسة هذا المُشكِل مِن أجْل إيجاد الحُلول المُمْكِنة،	16	rather we must have a national debate in order to study this problem in order to find possible solutions,
كما يجِب تَوْعِية الناس عن طريق برامِج تعليمية وعن طريق وسائِل الإِعْلام.	17	as well as educate people through educational programs and through the media.

Focus

The masdar (also known as a gerund or verbal noun) is negated by the noun عدم *absence/lack*, which precedes the masdar as the first element of an idafa construction. In other words, the negated masdar is عدم plus the masdar in the genitive case. This construction translates as *not __ing, un-__, dis-__, non-__,* etc.

Form the negative masdars and translate them.

positive masdar		negative masdar	
الاِسْتِطاعة	ability		
الاِكْتِراث	regard		
القِيام	doing		
الدَّفْع	payment		

Find examples of negative masdars in the text and write them below along with their translations.

عدم__	English

Answers: عدم اِحْتِرام الأَسْبَقية / non-payment عدم الدَّفْع / not doing عدم القِيام / disregard عدم الاِسْتِطاعة / inability عدم الاِسْتِطاعة / not respecting the right of way عدم إلْمام السّائقين / the lack of attention (inattention) to pedestrians عدم اِنْتِباهَ الرّاجِلين / both drivers and pedestrians عدم اِحْتِرام كُلّ مِن الرّاجِلين والسّائقين للإشارات الضَّوْئية / drivers not knowing traffic laws بقانون السَّيْر / not respecting traffic lights عدم الوعْي أَثْناء السِّياقة / not respecting stop signs عدم اِحْتِرام علامة قِف / inattention while driving

A Childhood Memory

Key Words

حِمار donkey   صلّاة prayer   عِقاب punishment

Main Idea

Abdulkarem tells us a story about ___.

   a. stealing a donkey
   b. running away from home
   c. locking his sister out of the house
   d. not coming home when he was supposed to

True or False

1. Abdulkarem and his friends stole a donkey from a neighbor's yard.
2. They rode the donkey all the way out of the city.
3. Abdulkarem's friends told his mom where he was.
4. Abdulkarem got a spanking from his mom.
5. Abdulkarem was late for lunch because he had lost track of time.

Multiple Choice

1. Abdulkarem and his friends stayed out playing past ___.

   a. the midday prayer   c. the sunset prayer
   b. the afternoon prayer   d. the night prayer

2. At the time of the midday prayer, children would usually ___.

   a. go home for lunch   c. go to school
   b. go to the mosque to pray   d. play in the streets

3. Who was worried about Abdulkarem: his father or his mother?

   a. his father   b. his mother   c. both   d. neither

4. Who opened the door for Abdulkarem?

   a. his father   b. his mother   c. his brother   d. his sister

5. Abdulkarem's friends' father was ___.

   a. an imam   b. a tailor   c. a merchant   d. dead

Matching

أُحِبّ أَنْ	again
لا يُمْكن أَنْ	even though
مَهْما	I remember
أَذْكُرُ	I still remember
في إِحْدى المَرّات	I would like to
عِنْدما	It's impossible that...
هذا بِمَثابة	no matter, whatever
بالرّغْم أَنّ	on one occasion
لا زِلْتُ أتذكّر	this amounts to
مرّة أُخْرى	to the point where...
بِحَيْث أَنّ	when

Answers

Main Idea: d **True or False:** 1. F[8] 2. T[9] 3. F[15-16] 4. T[22-23] 5. T[13] **Multiple Choice:** 1. a[11] 2. a[12] 3. c[16] 4. d[20] 5. c[24]

Matching: أُحِبّ أَنْ I would like to / لا يُمْكن أَنْ It's impossible that... / مَهْما no matter, whatever / أَذْكُرُ I remember / في
إِحْدى المَرّات on one occasion / عِنْدما when / هذا بِمَثابة this amounts to / بالرّغْم أَنّ even though / لا زِلْتُ أتذكّر I still
remember / مرّة أُخْرى again / بِحَيْث أَنّ to the point where...

Text

بِسْم الله الرّحْمن الرّحيم.	1	In the name of God the Merciful.
أُحِبّ أَنْ أتحدّث في هذا الـ... هذا اللِّقاء عن حَياة الطُّفولة.	2	I would like to talk at this... meeting [session] about childhood life.
الطُّفولة لِكُلِّ إِنْسان هِيَ الفِتْرة السّعيدة الّتي لَيْسَ فيها حِساب ولا عِقاب.	3	For everyone, childhood is a time free of accountability and punishment.
هُناك بعْض المُواقِف الّتي لا يُمْكن أَنْ تُمْحى مِن ذاكِرة الإنْسان مَهْما بلغَ مِنَ العُمُر.	4	[But] there are some situations that cannot be erased from a person's memory, no matter how old one is.
أَذْكُرُ بعْض الحَوَادِث الّتي حصلت لي عِنْدما كُنْتُ طِفلاً مَعَ جيرانِنا.	5	I remember some incidents with our neighbors that happened to me when I was a kid.
تعوّدْنا وإحْنا أطْفال صِغار أَنْ نلْعب بعْض الألْعاب الخفيفة في الحارة الّتي كُنّا نعيش فيها.	6	When we were young children, we used to play around in the quarter we lived in.
في إِحْدى المَرّات حصلت لنا حادِثة مَعَ... الحِمار،	7	On one occasion something happened with this donkey.

وهذا الحِمار الّذي كُنّا نلْعب بهِ في الحارة شرد وذهبَ إلى خارجِ الحارة الّتي كُنّا نعيش فيها.	8	The donkey we were playing in the neighborhood was roaming around and went out of the quarter we lived in.
وكُنّا نجْري وراءَهُ مِن شارعٍ إلى شارعٍ حتّى خرجَ إلى خارجِ المدينة	9	We were running after it from street to street, all the way out of the city.
وكُنّا نُلْحِقُهُ وكُنّا مجموعة مِنَ الأطْفال وأحدُنا يرْكبُ الحِمار والآخر يضْربُ الحِمار حتّى يجْري بِسُرْعة.	10	We, a group of kids, were following him. One of us was riding the donkey while another was hitting it to make it run faster.
ومضى بِنا الوقْت إلى أنْ أصْبحت السّاعة بعْدَ فترَة الظّهيرة أيّ بعْدَ صلَاة الظّهْر،	11	Time flew by into the afternoon, past the midday prayer time.
حَيْثُ أنّ... النّاس تعوّدوا في صلَاة الظّهْر أنْ يتِمّ أداء الصّلاة ويَعود جميع الـ... الأبْناء إلى بيُوتِهم لِتناوُلِ الغداء.	12	when people would perform the midday prayer and all the... children would go back to their homes for lunch.
في هذا اليَوْم كُنّا نلْعب معَ الحِمار وذهبْنا إلى خارجِ المدينة ولم نُدْرِك عن الوقْت أنّهُ يـ... يمُرُّ بِسرْعة.	13	[But] on that day, we were playing with the donkey and had gone out of the city and did not realize how quickly the time had... passed.
وعِنْدما عُدْنا إلى البَيْت وكانت والِدتي قد بحثت عنّي عن... في الشّوارِع والجوَامِع	14	When we got back to the house, my mother was looking for me... in the streets and mosques
وسألت من الاا... يلْعب معي أوْ مِنَ الأطْفال الّذينَ تعْرفُ أنّهُم مِن زُملائي يلْعبونَ معي في الحارة	15	and asking those who... played with me, or the kids that she knew that played with me in the neighborhood,
ولاكِن لا خبر فقلِقت والِدتي عنّي وكذلكَ والِدي.	16	but there was no news. And my mother was worried about me, as was my father.
فعُدْتُ إلى البَيْت ووجدْت أُمّي وهِيَ تصْرخ علَيَّ وتُصيح علَيَّ: لِماذا تأخّرْت عن مَوْعِد الغداء،	17	So I got back to the house and found my mom shouting at me and yelling at me, "Why were you late for lunch?"
فـ... لم تفْتح لي الباب لِلدُّخول إلى البَيْت	18	She wouldn't open the front door for me,
و... كان هذا بِمثابة عِقاب لي لِعدم اِحْترامي لِمَواعيد الغداء والعَوْدة إلى المنْزِل في الوَقْت المُحدّد الّذي كُنّا تربّيْنا علَيْه	19	and this amounted to a punishment for me for not respecting the lunch curfew or returning home at the designated time we had been raised with.
وحاوَلت أُخْتي الكُبْرى أنْ تقِف معي فنزلت إلى الباب وفتحت لي الباب	20	My older sister tried to stand with me, so she came down to the door and opened the door for me.
وقامت والِدتي بِصياح علَيها ونهْرِها لِماذا فتحت لي الباب.	21	And my mother shouted at her and reprimanded her [asking] why she'd opened the door for me.
و... لم أسْلم مِن ضرْبه أوْ ما يُقال علّقه.	22*	And... I didn't escape the beating, or what's called a spanking.
ضربتْني والِدتي لِتأخُّري بالرّغْم أنّها قد عاقبتْني بِعدم فتْح الباب لِأنّها أيْضًا قامت بِضربي	23	My mother hit me for being late, even though she had already punished me by not opening the door and also because she had shouted at me.

وكُنْتُ أتذكّر هذِه الحادثة معَ أبْناء الجيران حَيْث كان أحد الجيران مِن كُبار التُّجّار	24	And I remember this incident with my neighbors' sons, one of the big merchants.
و... لا زِلْتُ أتذكّرُها و... لم أُكرِّرْها في حَيَاتي مرّة أُخْرى	25	I still remember. I never did this again in my life,
وحافظْت على المَوْعِد للعَوْدة للبَيْت بعْدَ الصّلاة الـ... بعْدَ صلاة الظُّهْر وكذلِكَ بعْدَ صلاة المغْرب	26	and I kept to the time to be back home after the... midday prayer and also after the evening prayer,
بِحَيْث أنّني لا يُمْكِن أنْ أغيب على المنْزِل في هذِه الأوْقات وشُكْرًا.	27	to the point where I couldn't be away from home during these times. Thank you.

Notes

*22 علْقة is actually Yemeni dialect, the MSA word for which would be ضرْبًا مُبرِّحًا *a good spanking.*

A Childhood Memory

Key Words

عَيْب inappropriate; bad (manners)   الضِّيافة snacks (offered to guests)

Main Idea

Luma tells us about ___.

   a.   an embarrassing experience she had once at a tea party
   b.   how her mother used to make her diet as a child
   c.   why she didn't like going to tea parties with her mother
   d.   how daily tea parties led to becoming overweight as a child

True or False

   1.   Luma comes from a well-to-do family.
   2.   The tea parties were in the early afternoon.
   3.   Luma wasn't allowed to eat snacks at the tea parties.
   4.   Luma eventually told her mother how much she disliked going to the tea parties.
   5.   Luma's mother has since passed away.

Multiple Choice

   1.   The "ladies' daily visits", or tea parties, are called ___ in Jordan.

         a.   جلْسة *jalsa*^{t} b.   اِسْتِقْبال *istiqbal*   c.   زِيارة *ziyara*^{t} d.   حفْل *ħafl*

   2.   Luma's mother would bring Luma along to the tea parties because ___.

         a.   there was no one to watch her at home   c.   she didn't want to go alone
         b.   she wanted to teach her about manners   d.   Luma was afraid to stay home alone

   3.   When Luma's brother asked about the tea parties, Luma would ___.

         a.   lie and tell him how delicious the snacks were
         b.   start to cry out of frustration
         c.   tell him she wasn't allowed to have any snacks
         d.   ignore him

   4.   Luma had to go to the tea parties with her mom from age ___ to ___.

         a.   seven   b.   nine   c.   twelve   d.   fourteen

   5.   Luma's mother was very strict with her, ___.

         a.   and Luma was similarly strict with her own children
         b.   but Luma can now appreciate this
         c.   so Luma is even to this day timid about speaking her mind
         d.   but Luma wants her own children to speak their mind

Matching

MSA	LCA	English
أبي	عايْلة	but
إلى	أُبوْي	family
إلى البَيْت	نِحْنا	for me
أمامَ	سِت	home
اِمْرأة	زَيّ	in front of
تذهبُ	تْروح	in our country
جِدًّا	على	like; as
عائلة	عنّا	Lucky you!
عِنْدنا	كان فيه	my father
كان هُناكَ	ما كان فيه	not
لم تكُنْ تسْمحُ لي	للإلي	she goes
لم يكُنْ هُناكَ	بسّ	she wouldn't let me
لي	ما كانْت تخلّيني	such things
لَيْسَ	هَيْك أشياء	there was; there were
ماذا؟	قُدّام	there wasn't; there weren't
مِثْلَ	عالبَيْت	to
مِثْلَ هذِهِ الأشْياء	شو؟	very
نحْنُ	نْيالك	we
ولكِن	كْثير	what?
يا لحظّكَ	مِش	woman; lady
أيّ شخْص	على هالحال	and then
ثُمَّ	ما بدّي	anyone
لا أُريدُ	وساعتْها	I don't want
هكذا	يَوْميتْها	that day
يَوْمَئِذٍ	أيّ حدا	this way

Answers

Text

أنا البِنْت الوحيدة في العايْلة	1	I am the only girl in the family.
وعنْدي أخَيْن أكْبر منّي.	2	I have my two older brothers.
وكانوا أمّي وأبوْي كثير مبْسوطين عليّ	3	Father and mother were very happy to have me
ودايْمًا خايْفين عليّ.	4	and [they were] always very concerned for my safety.
ونحْنا عايْلة مُتَوسِّطة منْعيش مِن دخْل أبوْي	5*	We were a middle-class family and lived on the income of my father,
اِلّي كان بِشْتغل مُهنْدِس طُرُقات في أمانة العاصمة	6	who was road engineer working for the municipality of the capital city,
وكان معاشُه على قدُّه.	7	and his salary was barely enough.
طبْعًا أمّي سِتّ زيّ كُلّ السِّتات، كانت تْروح كُلّ يَوْم على جمْعات سِتّاتية،	8	Of course, my mother, like all the ladies, used to go on ladies' daily visits—
منْسمّيها عنّا في الأُرْدُنّ إسْتِقْبال.	9	in Jordan we call them *istiqbal*.
يَعْني تْروح السّاعة أرْبعة العصر وتْرْجع حَوالي السّاعة سبْعة مساءً.	10	So, she'd go at four in the afternoon and come back about seven in the evening.
وكان فيه... وكان ما فيه حدا يدير بالُه عليّ في البَيْت	11	There was... there wasn't anyone to take care of me at home,
فكانِت تاخُذْني معها.	12	so she would take me with her.
وطبْعًا كان هذا المفْروض يكون فُرْصة لإِلّي عشان أسْتمْتع بِوقْتي بالـ... بالزِّيارة اِلّي هيَ رايْحة علَيْها،	13	Of course, this should have been a chance for me to enjoy my time with the visit she was going on,
بسّ أُمّي الله يِرْحمْها كانت تخلّيني قاعْدة جنْبها طول فتْرة الزِّيارة	14	but my mother (God rest her soul) used to make me sit next to her during the whole visit,
وما كانْت تخلّيني لا أقوم ولا أتحّرك.	15	and she would neither let me stand nor move about.
وطبْعًا في الزِّيارة كانوا السِّتات بِضيّفوا عصير وكَيْك وشوكلاتة وكُلّ شَيْء زاكي.	16	Of course, during the visit the ladies would offer juice, cake, and chocolate, and all sorts of delicious things.
ولمّا بِجيوا يعْطوا الضّيافة لأُمّي ويِطْلُبوا إنّه أنا أخُذ مِن الضّيافة،	17	When they would come to give the snacks to my mom and offer me some of the snacks,
كانت أُمّي تِتْطلّع عليّ نظرة، يا لطيف، جدّية و... مِكشّرة. وإنّه لأ، عَيْب.	18	my mother (Oh my word!) would look at me with a very serious and firm look, scowling "No, it's bad manners!",
وتقول للنّاس: لا شُكْرًا،	19	and she would tell them, "No thank you.
ما فيه داعي.	20	That's not necessary.
هيَ ما بْتاكُل هَيْك أشْياء.	21	She does not eat such things."
وطبْعًا أنا أكون كثير جاي على بالي: أكُل،	22	And in my mind I was thinking, "I do eat them!

أُخُذ مِن الأشْياءِ اِللي بِيْضيِّفوها.	23	I'll take one of those things you're serving!"
وطبْعًا أظلّ ساكْتة وما أعْترض	24	Of course, I remained silent and did not object
لِأنّه عَيْب في حضارتْنا الاعْتِراض على كِلْمة الأُمّ خاصّةً قُدّام النّاس.	25	because it's (considered) bad in our culture to talk back to your mother, especially in front of others.
وتخْلص الزِّيارة ونُرْجع عالبَيْت	26	Then the visit would finish and we would go back home.
فيسْألْني أخُوي اِللي أكْبَر مِنّي: شو أكلْتوا؟	27	And my older brother would ask me what we had eaten.
أقُول لُه ضيِّفوا هَيْك وهَيْك وهَيْك، عصير وكَيْك وهدا.	28	I'd tell him they served us this and that... juice and cake and what not.
ويْقول لي: نيالَك، أكلْتي مِن كُلّها... مِن كُلّ هادي الأشْيا؟	29	And he'd say, "Lucky you! You ate all of... all of those things?"
وأقُول لأ، وأنا مُعَصبة لِأنّه أُمّي ما سمحت لي أخُذ	30	And I'd say, "No, and I'm so annoyed because mom wouldn't let me have any."
وأكون كِثير كِثير كِثير مغْيوظة.	31	And I was so, so, so angry.
طبْعًا نِحْنا عايْلة حالتْنا الماديّة مُتَوسِّطة وفي كِثير مِن الأحْيان كانوا اِللي عم بِيْضيِّفوا شَيْء ما فيه عنّا مِنُه بالبَيْت.	32	We were a middle class family and some of the things they used to offer us we'd rarely ever have at home,
بسّ مَوْقِف أُمّي ما عمرُه تغيَّر.	33	but my mother's stance would never change.
طبْعًا تِتْكرّر هادي العمليّة كُلّ يَوْم...	34	This (process) would repeat every day...
طبْعًا هذا الحكي كان مِن وقْت ما كان عُمْري سبْعة سْنين و... تِتْكرّر كُلّ يَوْم وأنا صُرْت ما أحُبّ أروح معَ أُمّي على الزِّيارات	35	the (same) story was from when I was seven years to the point where I didn't like going with my mom on the visits
لِأنّه مِش مسْموح لي أضيَّف زَيّ باقية الزُّوار.	36	because she wouldn't let me be treated like the other guests.
وظلّيْنا على هالحال لِصار عُمْري أرْبعْطشر سنة.	37	And we went on this way until I was fourteen.
يَوْم جمّعْت شجاعْتي ووقفْت قُدّام أُمّي قُلْت لها:	38	And then one day I gathered my courage and stood up and said,
أنا ما باحُبّ أروح معكي على هذِهِ الزِّيارات	39	"I don't like going on those visits with you,
وما بِدّي أروح.	40	and I don't want to go [anymore]."
فطبْعًا أُمّي ما عجبها المَوْضوع	41	Of course, my mother, she didn't like this situation,
وساعتْها تْناقشت معَ أبي	42	and then she discussed it with my father.
بالمَوْضوع وقرّروا إنّه ما فيه مانع أظلّ في البَيْت معَ إخوتي.	43	And they decided there was no reason I couldn't stay at home with my brothers.
يَوْميتها حسّيْت بالحُرّية	44	That day I felt free.
وصُرْت مِن وقْتها إذا ما بِيْعجِبْني شَيْء، أعْترِض وأقُول رأي بْصراحة	45	And from then on, if I didn't like something, I would object and speak my mind,
حتّى لَوْ إنّ الاعْتِراض ما بِيِعْجِب أُمّي وأبوْي.	46	even if my mom and dad didn't like my objecting.

كُنْت دائمًا أقول عانَيْت بِما فيه الكِفاية في صِغري مِن الكَبْت وعدم الضِّيافة.	47	I always say I've had enough of suppression and lack of snacks in my childhood.
والواقع ههه... هالتَّجْرِبة علمتْني... علمتْني إنّي ما أكْبِت ولادي.	48	Really, this experience taught me... taught me never to oppress my children,
أخَلّيهُم يِحْكوا رأيهُم ولا... و...	49	to let them say their opinion, nor to... and...
مِش بسّ ولادي حتّى أيّ حدا إنُّه يِحْكوا رأيهُم بصراحة	50	not only my children but everybody to speak their mind
وما أجْبِر ولادي يْروحوا معي زِيارات إذا ما... إذا ما بْحِبّوا.	51	and not to make my children go with me on visits if they don't want to.
فـ... الله يِرْحمْها أمّي كانت كثير كِثير شديدة	52	But, God rest her soul, my mother was so, so strict
وكانت كِثير كِثير تِهتمّ إنّه النّاس تِقول إنّه بِنْتها مُؤَدّبة وما بْتعْمل أيّ شَيْء عَيْب.	53	and it was very, very important for her that people say her daughter is polite and does not do anything ill-mannered.
ههه... الله يِرْحمْكي يا أمّي.	54	Ha-ha... God bless you, mom.
وبسّ... شُكْرًا.	55	And that's it. Thank you.

Notes

*5 Levantine Arabic, as many other dialects of Arabic, adds the prefix بـ b- to mark the present tense. However, the 1st person plural adds مـ instead.

Focus

The verb أَعْجَبَ، يُعْجِبُ appears in this segment in Luma's dialect as عجب، بيعْجِب on lines 41, 45, and 46. Write these in the left column of the table below. Then compare the subjects and objects in these examples to their English translations. Keep in mind that a verb may be followed by its subject in Arabic.

أَعْجَبَ	like	please
أمّي ما عجبها المَوْضوع	My mother, she didn't like this situation.	
إذا ما بْيِعْجِبني شَيْء	if I didn't like something...	
حتّى لَوْ إنّ الإعْتِراض ما بيِعْجِب أمّي وأبوْي	even if my mom and dad didn't like my objecting	

The subjects have been underlined in the table above. Notice that these correspond to the objects of the verb *like* in the English translations. Although *like* is a more natural translation, a more *direct* translation would use the verb *please*, which mirrors the subject and object in Arabic. *'I like it'* becomes *'it pleases me'*. Retranslate the sentences in the table using *please*.

Answers: (As for) my mother, the situation didn't please her. / if something didn't please me... / even if my objecting didn't please my mom and dad.

University

Key Words

مِنْهاج (مناهِجُ) curriculum   الحَياة الجامِعية university life

Main Idea

a. Walid discusses positive and negative aspects of student life at Lebanese universities.
b. Walid speaks highly of Lebanese universities and student life at them.
c. Walid has many complaints about Lebanese universities and suggestions for improving them.
d. Walid compares American, French, and Lebanese universities.

True or False

1. Lebanese universities have a mediocre reputation in the Arab world.
2. Government universities use Arabic, and not French or English, as the first language.
3. All Lebanese universities use the French curriculum nowadays.
4. Walid's university held extra-curricular educational activities for students.
5. Walid misses university life.

Multiple Choice

1. Which of the following languages are used as a first language in universities in Lebanon?

    a. Arabic   b. Farsi   c. English   d. French

2. Which of the following did Walid mention?

    a. Lebanese universities offer a wide range of majors.
    b. Professors at Lebanese universities come from all over the world.
    c. The Lebanese University has several campuses throughout the country.
    d. An American curriculum is used at some Lebanese universities.

3. Walid mentions that many major foreign universities offer scholarships ___.

    a. to Lebanese students to lecture at their universities
    b. to Lebanese students to study at their universities
    c. to their students to study at Lebanese universities
    d. *none of the above*

4. Walid implies that the relationship between students and university staff is ___.

    a. more formal than in the West   c. sometimes problematic
    b. quite hierarchical   d. amicable and harmonious

5. Thinking back to his days at university, Walid misses ___.

    a. the fear of failure   c. his professors
    b. the parties   d. *all of the above*

Matching

حَيْثُ تكون... أوْ...	(such) as
أمّا... فـ	a large number of
مِنْها	also
وغَيْرُها	always
في ما بَيْنها	among them
ذاتُ	and so on
فعدد كبير مِنَ الـ	as for...
بعْض الشَّيْء	either... or...
كما، كـ	from a standpoint of ___
كما أنّ	has
عادةً ما	in short
مِنَ النّاحِية الـ	including
لطالما	somewhat
باخْتِصار	usually

Answers

Main Idea: b **True or False:** 1. F[2] 2. T[4] 3. F[11] 4. T[18] 5. T[24-26] **Multiple Choice:** 1. a[4] & c[7] & d[7] 2. a[8] & d[11] 3. a[13] 4. d[16] 5. d[26-27] **Matching:** في ما بَيْنها among / وغَيْرُها and so on / مِنْها including / أمّا... فـ as for... / حَيْثُ تكون... أوْ... either... or... / عادةً ما usually / also كما أنّ / somewhat كما، كـ (such) as / بعْض الشَّيْء a large number of / فعدد كبير مِنَ الـ has ذاتُ / them / مِنَ النّاحِية الـ from a standpoint of ___ / لطالما always / باخْتِصار in short

Text

	#	
صباح الخَيْر. مَوْضوع اليَوْم هُوَ الجامِعات في لُبْنان والحَياة الجامِعية فيها.	1	Good morning. Today's topic is universities in Lebanon and university life at them.
تعْتبرُ الجامِعات اللُّبْنانية مِن أقْوى الجامِعات في الدُّوَل العربية،	2	Lebanese universities are considered to be among the top universities in the Arab world
وذلِكَ لِتمَيُّزِها بِتنوُّع اللُّغات المُعْتمِدة في التّدْريس.	3	for their distinction of diversity in languages used in teaching.
فاللُّغةُ العربية مثلًا هِيَ اللُّغة الأُمّ في الجامِعات الحُكومية أيْ الجامِعة اللُّبْنانية،	4	The Arabic language, for example, is the mother language in government universities, that is, the Lebanese University.

ثُمَّ تليها اللُّغة الثّانية حَيْثُ تكون الفرنْسيَّةُ أو الإنْكِليزية.	5	Then the second language follows, either French or English.
أمّا في الجامِعات الخاصّة فالوضْع يخْتلِفُ بعْض الشَّيْء	6	As for private universities, the situation is somewhat different,
ففي بعْض الجامِعات الخاصّة تكون اللُّغةُ العربيّةُ فيها اللُّغة الثّانية واللُّغةُ الأولى هِيَ الفرنْسية أوِ الإنْكِليزية.	7	for at some private universities, Arabic is the second language, and the first language is French or English.
أمّا الاخْتِصاصات المَوْجودة في لُبْنان فهِيَ جِدًّا مُتنوِّعة	8	The majors [specialties] present in Lebanon are very wide-ranging.
ويُمْكِنُنا القَوْل أنّها تشْمل جميعَ الاخْتِصاصات المَوْجودة عالميًا مِنها الطِّبّ، الهنْدسة، الإدارة العامّة، التّسْويق، الحُقوق وغَيْرها.	9	We could say these cover all of the majors found in the world, including medicine, engineering, public administration, marketing, law, and so on.
المِنْهاج المُدرَّس في الجامِعات اللُّبْنانية أيْضًا يخْتلِف في ما بَيْنها،	10	The curriculum at Lebanese universities also differs among them,
مِنْها ما يعْتمِد ويُدرَّس المِنْهاج الفرنْسي (يعْتمِد على عدد السِّنين ومُعدّل النّجاح) ومِنْها المِنْهاج الأَمْرْكي (أوْ مِنْهاج الـcredits والفُصول) ومِنْها مناهجُ أُخْرى.	11	including what the French curriculum teaches (which depends on the number of years and the success rate), the American curriculum (or the curriculum of credits and semesters), and other curricula.
أمّا مِن ناحية الشُّهْرة العالمية، فالجامِعات اللُّبْنانية ذاتُ سُمْعةً أكْثر مِن مُمْتازة عالميًا.	12	In terms of international renown, Lebanese universities have a more than excellent reputation globally.
فعدَدٌ كبير مِنَ الجامِعات الأجْنبية الكُبْرى تُقدِّمُ مِنحًا مدْرسيةً هامّة للتّلاميذ اللُّبْنانيون للعمل كمُعيِّدين في هذِهِ الجامِعات الكُبْرى	13	A large number of major foreign universities offer significant scholarships for Lebanese students to work as lecturers at these major universities,
والبعْض الآخر يسْعى لإبْرام عُقود مُبادلة الطَّلبة معَ الجامِعات اللُّبْنانية.	14	and others seek to enter into agreements to exchange students with Lebanese universities.
أمّا حَياةُ الطَّلبة في الجامِعات اللُّبْنانية فتخْتلِفُ بعْض الشَّيْء عن باقي الدُّوَل،	15	The lives of the students in Lebanese universities differ somewhat from the rest of the world.
حَيْثُ يسودُها رقابة صحّية وَاجْتِماعية دائمة على الطُّلاب، كما المحبّة المُتبادلة والصَّداقة بَيْنَ الطُّلاب والمُدرِّسون والهيْئة الإدارية	16	Continual social and health control for students is prevalent, as is mutual love and friendship between students, teachers, and the administration,
وتشْجيع دائِم للطُّلاب لتكْمِلة دِراستِهم والابْتِعاد عنِ المُضِرّات	17	as well as continual encouragement for students to supplement their studies and stay away from hazards
كالمُخْدرات والإفْراط في الكُحول حَيْثُ تُقام ندَواتٌ ومُحاضرات للتّوْعية العامّة.	18	such as drugs and excessive alcohol, for which seminars and lectures are held to educate the public.
كما أنَّ في كُلّ جامِعة هَيْئةٌ طُلابية تُمثِّل الطُّلاب في المُطالبة	19	Also, at every university there is a student body that represents students' demands,

والدِّفاع عن حُقوقِهِم، تنْظيم النَدَوات، المُناسبات والحفلات الطُّلابية.	20	defends their rights, organizes seminars, events, and student parties.
هذِهِ المُناسبات والحفلات عادةً ما تكون رياضية أوْ تعارُف للطُّلاب الجُدُد.	21	These events and parties are usually for sports or to get to know new students.
أمّا عن تجْربتي الخاصّة في الجامِعات اللُّبنانية، فأكادُ أجْزِم أنّها مِن أفضل مراحِل حَياتي،	22	As for my own experience at Lebanese universities, I can assure you it was one of the best times of my life,
لَيْسَ مِنَ النّاحية العِلْمية فقط إِنّما مِنَ النّاحية الأخْلاقية والاجْتِماعية أيْضًا.	23	not only educationally, but ethically and socially, as well.
أتمّنى العَوْدة إلى تِلْكَ المرْحلةِ والجامعة،	24	I wish I could go back to that time and the university,
إلى تِلْكَ الحَياة الطُّلابية الّتي لطالما شعرْتُ أنّني أدْرُس بَيْنَ إخْواني وأخَواتي.	25	to that student life in which I always felt I was studying among my brothers and sisters.
اِشْتقْتُ إلى الخَوْفِ مِنَ الفشل وإلى تِلْكَ الحفلات والتّحدِّيات الرِّياضية،	26	I miss the fear of failure and to those parties and sporting challenges,
إلى الصداقة الشّبابية بَيْننا، إلى الأساتِذة الّذينَ أعْطوا كُلَّ ما لدَيْهُم لأجْلِنا.	27	the youthful friendships among us, the professors who gave their all for us.
اممم... باخْتِصار هذِهِ هِيَ الحَياة الجامِعية في لُبْنان.	28	Um... In short, this is college life in Lebanon.

Hijab

Razanne (Syria)
MSA 466 words (88 wpm)
13

Key Words

الحِجاب the hijab	مُحجِّبة covered; wearing a hijab	اِرْتدى (يرْتدي) to wear
غِطاء headscarf	مفْروض على imposed on; required for	

Main Idea

Razanne tells us about ___.

a. why she's chosen not to wear the hijab in the United States.
b. being interviewed about wearing the hijab for a local newspaper in the U.S.
c. discrimination she's felt in the United States as a hijab-wearing Muslim woman.
d. times she's answered American women's questions about the hijab.

True or False

1. In America, Razanne is often asked about the hijab.
2. Razanne wears the hijab more out of habit than religious piety.
3. Razanne is married.
4. Razanne wears the hijab both at home and in public.
5. Razanne seems to think the strangers who asked her questions were a bit rude.

Multiple Choice

1. In Islam, the hijab is imposed on ___.

   a. girls from the age of six or seven
   b. young women from the age of sixteen or seventeen
   c. married women
   d. widowed women

2. Razanne explained that the hijab is ___.

   a. an obligation   b. optional   c. a sign of piety   d. a cultural tradition

3. At home, Razanne might wear ___.

   a. a headscarf
   b. a wig
   c. shorts and a tank top
   d. *none of the above*

4. One young woman thought Razanne wore a headscarf because ___.

   a. her husband forced her to
   b. she was bald
   c. she was a religious fanatic
   d. she liked drawing attention to herself

5. Razanne feels that a woman's ___ should be kept from strange men and reserved for her husband.

   a. hair   b. body   c. beauty   d. *all of the above*

Matching

باعْتِبار أنّ	anywhere
أيّ مكان	approximately; about
مرّة	certainly; for sure
مُنْذُ أنْ	given that...; as
تقْريبًا	have the right to...
مِن حقِّهِ أنْ	I can...
أكْثر مِمّا مضى	I hope that...
في هذا الزّمن	I want to...
بالتّأْكيد	in case
أريد أنْ	nowadays
بإمْكاني أنْ	one time; on one occasion...
في حال	since; from the time
أتمنّى أنّ	than ever; than in the past

Answers

Main Idea: d **True or False:** 1. T[2] 2. F[14] 3. T[29] 4. F[25,28] 5. F[30-31,43] **Multiple Choice:** 1. b[7] 2. a[14] 3. c[25-27] 4. b[35] 5. d[15,41]

Matching: باعْتِبار أنّ given that...; as / أيّ مكان anywhere / مرّة one time; on one occasion... / مُنْذُ أنْ since; from when / في هذا الزّمن approximately; about / مِن حقِّهِ أنْ have the right to... / أكْثر مِمّا مضى than ever; than in the past / تقْريبًا nowadays / بالتّأْكيد certainly; for sure / أريد أنْ I want to... / بإمْكاني أنْ I can... / في حال in case / أتمنّى أنّ I hope that...

Text

الآن سأتحدّث عن مَوْضوع الحِجاب باعْتِبار أنّني فتاة مُسْلِمة مُحجّبة.	1	Now, I'm going to talk about hijab as a hijab-wearing Muslim young woman.
أعيش في أمَيْركا. فأنا أتعرّض للكثير مِنَ الأسْئِلة في الطّريق أوْ في السّوق أوْ في العمل أوْ أيّ مكان.	2	I live in America, so I am confronted with many questions in the street or in the marketplace or at work or anywhere.
اااه... سـ... سأقوم بالكلام عن بعْض هذِهِ المَواقِف الّتي تعرّضْت لها والأسْئِلة.	3	Uh... I... I will be talking about some of these situations that I have come across and the questions.
وأجيب... وأجيب أيْضًا عن هذِهِ الأسْئِلة.	4	I'll... I'll also answer these questions.
اممم... مرّة كُنْتُ في السّوق فجاءت إلَيّ الااه... سيّدة اممم... مُتوسّطة العُمْر	5	Um... one time I was in the market and uh... a middle-aged lady came up to me

اممم... وسألتْني... ااه...: متى يُفْرض علَيْكُم لِبْس الحِجاب في ااه... الإسْلام؟	6	um... and asked me... uh... "When is the hijab imposed on you in uh... Islam?"
عِنْدها أنا أجبْتُها أنَّ الحِجاب هُوَ مفْروض على كُلِّ امْرأة مُنْذُ أنْ تصِل إلى سِنِّ البُلوغ، يعْني حَوالي سِتّة عشر أوْ سَبْعة عشر سنة.	7	I then replied that the hijab is imposed on every woman from the time she reaches young adulthood, meaning about sixteen or seventeen years old.
فهِيَ قالت: أنا أرى بعض البنات عادةً يلْبِسونَ الحِجاب ولكن لَيْسوا صِغارًا.	8*	Then she said, "I see some girls who usually wear the hijab but are not little.
كُلُّهُم في ااه... هذِهِ الأعْمار تقْريبًا.	9	All of them uh... are around that age.
الصِّغار لَيْسَ مفْروض علَيْهِم؟	10	It's not imposed on the young ones?"
فأنا أجبْتُها: لا، غَيْر مفْروض علَيْهِم. ااه... وذهبت.	11	I answered, "No, it's not imposed on them." Uh... and then she went away.
مرّة أُخْرى جاءت اِمْرأة سألتْني لِماذا ترْتدين غِطاء الرَّأس؟	12	Another time, a woman came up and asked me, "Why do you wear a headscarf?"
فأنا قُلْتُ لها ااه...: هذا يُدْعى حِجاب في الإسْلام وهُوَ...	13	I told her, "This is called hijab in Islam, and it...
وأنا أرْتديه لِأنَّني مُسْلِمة وهُوَ فرْض في الإسْلام	14	and I wear it because I am a Muslim and it's an obligation in Islam
اممم... لكَيْ تسْتُري جِسْمكِ وتُغطّي الجُزْء الأكْبر مِن جمالكِ فقط وتحْفظيها لِزَوْجكِ.	15	hmm... so that you veil your body and just cover the majority of uh... your beauty and keep it for your husband.
أمّا الرِّجال الغُرباء فـ... ااه... لَيْسَ مِن حقِّهِم أنْ يروا هذِهِ الأُمور عِنْدكِ.	16	Men who are strangers have no right to see these things you have."
فهِيَ قالت: أوه، هذا، هذا جميل وهُوَ... أنا مُتأكِّدة أنَّهُ صعْب في هذا الوقْت	17	Then she said, "Oh, that's nice. And it... I'm sure it is difficult at this time
لِأنَّ جميع النِّساء أوْ أغْلب النِّساء يتسابقْنَ لِأنْ يكْشِفْنَ عن أجْسادِهِنَّ أكْثر مِنَ الـ... أكْثر مِن ااه... مِمّا مضى في هذا الزّمن.	18	because all women, or most women, are in a race to bare more of their bodies than... than... ever nowadays.
فبِالتّأكيد هُوَ شَيْء صعْب، ما تقومينَ بِه أنّكِ تسْترين جِسْمكِ.	19	Is certainly a difficult thing you're doing, covering up your body."
فقُلْتُ لها: بِالتّأكيد ولكِن ااه... المَوْضوع صعْب في بِدايتِه ولكِن ثُمَّ بعْدَ ذلِك يُصْبِح أكْثر سُهولة.	20	I said to her, "Certainly, but uh... it's difficult in the beginning, but then it becomes easier."
ااه... مرّة أُخْرى أيْضًا جاءت... جاءت لِعِنْدي اِمْرأة وسألتْني:	21	Uh... and another time, a woman came uh... came up to me and asked me,
هل ترْتدينَ الحِجاب أوْ هذا الغِطاء ااه... في البَيْت، في بَيْتِك؟	22	"Do you wear a hijab, or headscarf, hmm... at home, in your house?"
قُلْتُ لها: لا. فقالت وسألتْني:	23	I told her no. And she said... she asked me,
هل ترْتدينَ ااه... هذا اللِّباس أمام زَوْجِك؟	24	"Do you wear these clothes around your husband?"

فقُلْتُ لها: لا، أنا أرْتدي مِثْلِك في البَيت... مِثْلِك في البَيت.	25*	I said to her, "No, I dress like you at home... like you at home."
فهِيَ قالت لي... فهِيَ كانت تلْبِس ااااه... ثِياب عادية ااااه... سِرْوال قصير و... ااااه... ولِباس صَيْفي	26	She said to me uh... she was wearing regular clothes, uh... shorts and uh... and summer clothes,
يعْني اممم... مِثْلَ shorts and tank top	27	you know, hmm... like "shorts and a tank top"
اممم... فأنا قُلْتُ لها حينها: لا، أنا ألْبِس مِثْلَ ما أنْتِ تلْبِسين في البَيت.	28	Hmm... I told her then, "No, I dress like what are you are wearing at home.
ااااه.. ولكِن لا ألْبِس هذا... هذا اللِّباس أمامَ الرِّجال الغُرباء، فقط أمام زوْجي.	29	Uh... but I don't wear these clothes in front of strange men, just in front of my husband."
فهِيَ قالت لي: شُكْرًا ولكِن كُنْتُ فقط أُريد أن أسأل هذا السُّؤال مُنْذ زمن وشُكْرًا لكِ علىالإجابة.	30*	She said to me, "Thank you, but I've just wanted to ask this question for a long time, and thank you for answering."
طبْعًا قُلْتُ لها: أهْلًا وسهْلًا.	31	Of course I told her, "You're welcome."
ومرّة أخْرى واحِدة مِنَ الفتَيات سألتْني: أُريد	32	One other time, a girl asked me, "I want to"...
ااااه... قالت لي: أُريد أنْ أسألكِ سُؤالًا.	33	uh... she said to me, "I want to ask you a question."
قُلْتُ لها: تفضّلي.	34	I told her, "Go ahead."
قالت لي: هل أنْتِ ترْتدينَ غِطاء الرّأس لِأنَّ لَيْسَ لدَيْكِ شعْر؟	35	She said to me, "Are you wearing a headscarf because you don't have any hair?"
فقُلْتُ لها حينها اممم...: لا، أنا لدَيَّ شعْر وشعْري جميل	36	So I told her then, hmm... "No, I have hair and my hair is beautiful.
وبإمْكاني أنْ أُريكِ شعْري إذا أحْببْتِ	37	Uh... and I can show my hair, if you'd like.
ولكِن لا أسْتطيع... لا أحِبّ أنْ أُريه إلى كُلّ النّاس.	38	But I can't and I don't like to show it to everyone."
فهِيَ عِنْدها سألتْني: لِماذا؟	39	She then asked me why.
قُلْتُ لها نفس الجَواب تقْريبًا:	40	I told her the same answer, more or less,
لِأنَّني أُخْفي هذِه الأُمور الجمالية في جِسْمي وشعْري وهذِه الأُمور كُلّها أُخْفيها وأخبِّئُها فقط لِـ... ااااه... لِزوْجي.	41	"Because I hide these aesthetic things of my body and my hair and all these things, and reserve them only for my husband.
لا أُريد جميع النّاس أنْ يرَوْنها.	42	I do not want everyone to see them.
ااااه... طبْعًا تشكّرتْني على هذِه المعْلومة.	43	Uh... of course she thanked me for this information.
يعْني أنا هذِه تقْريبًا الأسْئِلة الّتي أتذكّرُها.	44	I mean, these are the questions, more or less, as I remember them.
اممم... في حال كُنْتُم تتساءلونَ نفْس الأسْئِلة فأتمَنّى أنَّكُم قد حصلتُم على الأجْوِبة المُناسبة.	45	Um... in case you're wondering the same questions, I hope you 've been given adequate answers.

Notes

*9 Here, the feminine plural يلْبِسْنَ should have been used. Most dialects, such as Razanne's, replace the feminine plural with the masculine plural, and so it is common to see native speakers failing to use the feminine plural correctly.

*25 Razanne first used the masculine form of the suffix كَ *you* by mistake, so she corrected herself.

*30 عالإجابة is a contracted form of على الإجابة. While it is not considered correct in written MSA, it is quite common in speech.

Poverty in Yemen

Key Words

الفقْر poverty	طبقة (social) class
دخْل income	صرفَ، يصْرف spend

Main Idea

    a. Abdulkarem focuses on the various causes of poverty in his country.
    b. Abdulkarem focuses on the solutions to poverty in his country.
    c. Abdulkarem compares Yemen's situation to that of neighboring countries.
    d. Abdulkarem focuses on a single cause of the poverty in Yemen.

True or False

    1. Poverty is a serious problem in Yemen.
    2. There used to be three social classes, but now there are just two.
    3. Some poor spend too much on chewing qat instead of on their families.
    4. Some families that are better off help out their poorer neighbors.
    5. Abdulkarem talks about his own family's financial struggles.

Multiple Choice

1. According to Abdulkarem, the poverty rate in Yemen is now ___ percent.

    a. 40   b. 45   c. 50   d. 55

2. Which of the following is **not** mentioned as a cause of poverty?

    a. a rise in the cost of living   c. migration into cities
    b. corruption   d. the return of workers from Gulf states

3. Farmers leave their land and migrate to cities because ___.

    a. there isn't enough water to farm successfully
    b. there are better jobs there
    c. the government encourages this migration
    d. the government no longer offers farm subsidies

4. Some unemployed people resort to ___.

    a. selling drugs   b. selling sex   c. stealing   d. *all of the above*

5. The government offers welfare to needy families in the form of ___.

    a. 3,000 rials once every three months
    b. 3,000 rials once every month
    c. 30,000 rials once every two months
    d. 30,000 rials once every month

Matching

MSA	YCA	English
الآن	نِبْسِر إنّ	he has; his, of him
جِدًّا	حقّه	is just
كانَ يوجد	يلّا يِكاد يِكون	now
لا يزالُ	كان زمان هناك	she doesn't have
لهُ، ـهُ	ذا الحين	still
لَيْسَ لها	ما عد	there used to be
مُجرّد، فقط	قَوي	they work
نرى أنَّ	يِشْتِغْلوا	very
يَعْملونَ	ما بِش معها	we see that...

Answers

Main Idea: a **True or False:** 1. T[4] 2. F[14] 3. T[20] 4. T[30-31] 5. F **Multiple Choice:** 1. b[10] 2. b[11,24-26] 3. a[21-22] 4. d[27] 5. a[28-29]

Matching: نِبْسِر إنّ we see that... / نرى أنَّ / حقّه he has; his, of him / يلّا يِكاد يِكون / لهُ، ـهُ is just / كان زمان هناك / مُجرّد، فقط there now / يَعْملونَ / ما بِش معها they work جِدًّا / يِشْتِغْلوا / قَوي very لا يزالُ still / ذا الحين now كانَ يوجد الآن / ما عد / she doesn't have used to be لَيْسَ لها / ذا الحين

Text

مرْحبًا بِكُم مِن جديد.	1	Hello to you again.
عنْحاكى اليوم عن موضوع يِهمّ كُلّ يَمَني:	2*	Today we'll talk about a subject matter that's important to every Yemeni:
وهُوَ الفقْر والعَوَز في مُجْتمعْنا.	3	poverty and destitution in our society.
هذا الفقْر يُعْتبر ااه... مرض قَوي قَوِي على المُجْتمع اليَمني ويِأثِّر على كُلّ أُسْرة الّذي حقّها الدخْل قليل وما تِسْتطيعْش إنّها تُواجِه المصاريف حقّ هذا الزّمان	4①*	This poverty is considered uh... a very serious malady of Yemeni society and affects every family that has low income and cannot meet the expenses of these times,
بِحَيْث إنّه كُلّ واحِد يِسْتطيع إنّه يُنْفِّق على نفْسِه الأشياء الضّرورية.	5	so that everyone could earn [enough] for the necessities.
لكِن لَوْ جينا نِبْسِر إنّ الواحِد حقّه المعاش يلّا يِكاد يِكون يِكفّيه ويِصْرفِه في ااه... ماء وكهْرباء وتلفون،	6	But (if we come,) we see that one's salary is just enough to pay [spend on] uh... water, electricity, telephone,
إذا كان معِه تلفون و... وموادّ غِذائية الضّرورية جِدًّا.	7	if they have a telephone, and the most essential foodstuffs.
لِذلِك نِبْسِر إنّ مِسْتوى دخْل الواحِد لا يتناسِب مع مصْروفاتِه،	8	Therefore, we see that the level of one's income is not commensurate with his expenses,

يعْني إنّ به هناك فجْوة كبيرة ما بَيْن الدّخْل و... والصّرْف.	9	that is, that there is a big gap between income and... expenditures.
و... أسْباب الفقْر في اليَمن كثيرة. وقد وصلت نِسْبة الفقْر في بلادْنا إلى خمْسة وأرْبعين في المئة.	10	And... there are many reasons for poverty in Yemen. The poverty rate in our country has reached forty-five percent.
ااه... مِن أسْباب الفقْر ااه... ارْتِفاع نِسْبة الغلاء في الـ... في المعيشة وهِجْرة النّاس مِن الرّيف إلى المدينة	11①	Uh... Among the causes of poverty are uh... a rise in the... in the cost of living and the migration of people from the countryside to the city.
وهُم بيْتْركوا حقّهُم الأرْض ويخلّوها بور ويهِجْروها ولا يزْرعوها ولا شيء	12	They leave their land and leave it uncultivated and abandon it and don't cultivate it or anything.
وأيْضًا ظ... سبب ثاني ظُهور فجْوة ما بَيْن طبق الأغْنِياء والطبّقة الـ... والطّبّقة المُتوسِّطة.	13	Also... another reason is the emergence of a gap between the upper class and the... middle class.
كان زمان هُناك طبقتَيْن. ذا الحين ما عد باقي إلّا قدنا ثلاث طبقات:	14	There used to be two classes. But now, there are three classes:
طبقة الفُقراء جدًا وطبّقة ذَوي الدّخْل المحْدود وطبقة الـ... الأشْخاص الّذين هُم مُعْدِمين قوي.	15	the very poor, the low-income class, and the class of... people who are extremely destitute.
فالمُجْتمع عِنْدنا إلى... إلى عام ألف وتِسْعِمئة وتِسعين كان طبقتَيْن، أمّا الآن أصْبح ثلاث طبقات.	16	Until nineteen-ninety, we had a society of two classes, but now this has become three classes.
ومِن... ومِن الأسْباب الثّانية الّتي تِسبِّب ااه... للفقْر، عدم توازن في الدخْل والإنْفاق	17	And... another thing that has caused uh... poverty is the income disparity and expenses,
لأنّ الأُسْرة، مِثْل ما قُلْت في البِداية، معها ااه... دخْل وبعْضهُم معه المعاش حقّه	18	because a family, as I said at the beginning, has an uh... income, some people have their salary,
وبعْضهُم مِن ما يِكْتسِب إذا كان نجّار أوْ حدّاد ولا خيّاط ولا تاجِر فـ... ما بـ... الشّيْء الّذي بِيكْسِبه يلّا يكاد يكون يعْني يـ... يُوازي لِما يُصْرِفه له ولِأوْلاده.	19	and some from what they earn if they're a carpenter, blacksmith, tailor, or merchant. So... what... what a person earns might just be... that is, e... equivalent to what he spends on his children.
أمّا إذا كان مِخزّن فهذِه هيَ الطّامّة الكُبْرى لأنّه المخزّن يُصْرِف مبالغ كبيرة لِنفْسه ويـ... يِحْرِم أوْلاده مِنْها.	20	But if he is chews [qat], this is a great disaster because a [qat] chewer will spend large amounts on himself, and... his children will be deprived because of it.
أيْضًا مِن المشاكِل الثّانية جفاف الأراضي الزّراعية	21	Another problem is the dryness of farmland,
وهذا سبّب أنْ أصْحاب الأراضي الزّراعية تركوا أراضيهُم ودخلوا إلى... إلى المُدُن.	22	which has causes owners of agricultural land to leave their land and move to... to the cities.

اِنْتَقَلوا مِن الرّيف إلى المدينة. وهذا الظّاهِرة بِتْخَلّي ااااه... النّاس يِحِسّوا بإِنّ هؤُلاء النّاس الّذي بِيِجوا مِن الرّيف بِيأَثّروا عَلَيْهُم وياكُلوا مِن خَيْرات ما هُوَ مَوْجود ويِسَبِّبوا في غ... في نِسْبة غَلاء الأَسْعار.	23	They've moved from the countryside to the city, and this phenomenon makes uh... [city] people to feel that these people who come from rural areas will affect them and eat from the bounties of what is available and cause a rise in... in prices.
أَيْضًا ظاهِرة عَوْدة المُهاجِرين الّذين خرجـ... رجعوا مِن السّعودية ومِن دُوَل الخليج.	24	Another phenomenon is the return of migrants who went... [who] have returned from Saudi Arabia and the Gulf states.
هؤُلاء الأَشْخاص أَيْضًا كان سـ... سبب وجيه لِارْتِفاع ظاهِرة الفَقْر،	25	These people have also been a significant c... cause for the increase in the phenomenon of poverty,
حَيْث إِنّ بعْضهُم لَم يَجِد أَعْمال يِعْملْها في اليَمَن فلجَؤوا إلى ااااه... إِنّهُم يِشْتغْلوا في... في أَعْمال سيِّئة	26	since some of them haven't found jobs to do in Yemen and resort to... working in bad jobs
مِثل بَيْع الخُمور وبَيْع المُخَدِّرات وظاهِرة الجِنْس و... أَيْضًا ظاهِرة اللّجوء إلى السّرِقة وغَيْرِها وهذِه أَثّرت على المُجْتمع.	27	such as selling alcohol and selling drugs and (the phenomenon of) sex, and also (the phenomenon of) resorting to theft and so on, which impact the community.
فـ... الآن الدّوْلة بِتحاوِل إِنّها تِحِدّ مِن ظاهِرة الفَقْر وتِتْصُرّف لِبعْض الأُسَر المُعْوِزة والفقيرة الّتي ما بِش معها يعْني مبْلغ يِصِل إلى ثلاث أَلف رِيال،	28*	So... now the state is trying to limit (the phenomenon of) poverty by giving to some needy and poor families--who don't have anything, I mean--an amount of up to three thousand rials,
ومال تاخُذه الأُسْرة إلى بعد ثلاثة أَشْهُر، يعْني تُنْتظُر ثلاثة أَشْهُر لما تُصْرَف لها الدّوْلة.	29	which families take every three months, that is, you wait for three months to get the money.
وحالتْهُم فُقراء ولكِن هُناك أَيْضًا التّكافُل الاِجْتِماعي عِنْدَ بعْض الأُسَر الّذي حالتْها جيِّدة.	30	They're poor, but there's also social cooperation in some families whose situation is good.
بِتْصُرّف على بعْض الأُسَر الفقيرة في الأَحْياء والشّوارِع القريبة فيما بَيْناتْهُم البَيْن.	31	They give to some poor families in the neighborhoods and streets close by.
و... هُناك إِمْكانية لِلتّعاوُن بـ... بَيْن النّاس... فيما بَيْنهُم ونِتمنّى إِنّه يِتِمّ ما نقولْش إِنّه يِنْهَوْا الفَقْر	32	And... there is the possibility of cooperation b... between people... amongst themselves. And we hope to, let's not say 'end' poverty,
ولكِن يِخفِّفوا مِن ظاهِرة الفَقْر في بِلادْنا والله والله المُوفِّق وشُكْرًا.	33	but to lesson (the phenomenon of) poverty in our country. God bless and thank you.

Notes

*2 The future tense prefix in YCA is ﻋـ, except for the 1st person singular, for which it is ﺷـ. (MSA: ﺳـ ﺳَﻮْﻓَ)

ⓘ4 An excellent video on the dire situation in Yemen (in English and the Yemeni dialect with subtitles): **youtu.be/TBO0sPVSmBw**

*4 The negative is formed by sandwiching a verb (or particle) with ﻣﺎ....ﺶ.

ⓘ11 Corruption is considered by many to be another major cause of poverty in Yemen: **cnn.it/1rMX8k5**

*28 Three thousand Yemeni rial is approximately equivalent to 14 US dollars.

Transportation

Alaa (Egypt)
MSA 506 words (98 wpm)
●15

Key Words

(وسائل) وسيلة mode, means   مُواصلة transportation   فضّلَ، يُفضّل to prefer

Main Idea

a. Alaa explains how transportation has changed over the last century in Alexandria.
b. Alaa compares buses and trains to air travel in Egypt.
c. Alaa explains various modes of transportation in Alexandria as well as intercity travel in Egypt.
d. Alaa explains various modes of transportation in Alexandria only.

True or False

1. The tram in Alexandria has a women-only section.
2. There are both air-conditioned and non-air-conditioned city buses in Alexandria.
3. Alexandria has a subway system.
4. If you have a lot of luggage, it is better to take the train rather than the "Super Jet".
5. Microbuses are prone to accidents.

Multiple Choice

1. The safest and cheapest means of transportation in Alexandria is ___.

    a. taxis   c. the tram
    b. tuk-tuks   d. the bus

2. The "tuk-tuk" is ___.

    a. used in poorer areas
    b. a means of transportation imported from Thailand
    c. now more popular than taxis in Alexandria
    d. found on the streets of Cairo, but not Alexandria

3. Which means of transportation does Alaa mention?

    a. airplanes   b. camels   c. ferry boats   d.   motorcycles

4. The "Super Jet" is ___.

    a. an intercity bus   c. the Alexandria ferry boat system
    b. a low-cost airline   d. the first-class express train between Alexandria and Cairo

5. Alaa prefers the train to the intercity bus whenever possible because ___.

    a. it's cheaper   c. the show movies on a TV screen
    b. of its high speed d. the journey is enjoyable

Matching

في البِداية	a couple of years ago
كما قُلْت	according to
خاصةً	also; too
مُؤَخَّرًا	as I said
ما يُطْلَقُ علَيْهِ بِـ	by its very nature
كما... أيْضًا	due to
البعْض... والبعْض الآخر...	especially
يوجد	I had to
عِنْدما	in the beginning
مُنْذُ عِدّةِ سنوات	instead of
بِالطّبْع	of course
حسب	recently
أحْيانًا	some (people)... and others...
في حدِّ ذاتِها	sometimes
بِسبب	there is; there are
كُنْتُ مُضطرّة إلى أنْ	what is called; so called
عِوضًا عنِ	when

Answers

Text

سَأُحَدِّثُكُم اليَوم عن وسائلِ المُواصلات في الإسكندرية	1*	I will talk to you today about means of transportation in Alexandria,
وهِيَ المدينة الّتي اااه... أعيشُ فيها.	2	(which is) the city I... I live in.
اااه... هُناكَ وسائلُ كثيرةً اااه... هُناكَ وسائلُ كثيرةٌ جدًّا في مدينة الإسكندرية	3	Uh... there are a lot of means of transportation... Uh... There are very many means of transportation in the city of Alexandria,
ولكن أشهرُها وأقدمُها اااه... وأكثرُها اااه... عراقةً هُوَ التّرام!	4	but the most famous, oldest and antiquated (of them), is the tram!
اااه... ذلك لِأنَّهُ اااه... مُنذُ القدم اااه... يعني... وسيلةٌ مُواصلاتٍ قديمةٌ جِدًّا اااه... وأكثرُهُم أمانًا وأرخصُهُم أَيْضًا؛	5*	Uh... That is because uh... ever since olden times... I mean, it is a very old means of transportation, and the safest and also the cheapest (of them);
لِأنَّها تنْقسِمُ إلى عربةِ عائلاتٍ وعربةِ رِجالٍ وعربةِ سيِّدات.	6	as it is divided into one car for families, a car for men, and a car for women.
فمثلًا عِنْدَما كُنْتُ صغيرةً كُنْتُ أركبُ التّرامَ اااه... في البِداية،	7	So for example, when I was young, I would get on the tram uh... in the beginning,
لِأنِّي أَعْرِفُ المُحطّاتِ وكان أمانًا لِأنَّهُ اااه... كما قُلْت، ينْقسِمُ إلى عربةِ سيِّداتٍ وعربةِ رِجال.	8	as I knew the stations, and it was safe because, uh... as I said, it is divided into a wagon for women and a wagon for men.
اااه... يوجدُ أَيْضًا التاكسي (سيّارة الأُجرة) وهُوَ أكثرُهُم تكْلِفةً خاصةً "تاكسي العاصمة" وهُوَ ما يُمْكِنُ طلبِهِ بالهاتف.	9*	Uh... There is also the taxi, which is the most expensive, especially the "City Cab", which you can get by a phone call.
اااه... كما توجد.. اااه... الأوتوبيسات أوْ "الحافِلات" باللُّغة العربية الفُصحى وتنْقسِمُ إلى الأوتوبيسات العامّة، والأوتوبيسات المُكيَّفة.	10	Uh... also, there are the buses, or "ḥāfilāt" in Standard Arabic, and they are divided into general buses, and air-conditioned ones.
ومُؤَخّرًا مُنذُ اااه... بِضعةِ سنواتٍ ظهر اااه... ما يُطْلقُ علَيْه بالـ"فاسْت باص"	11	And recently, uh... a couple of years ago, a so called "Fast Bus" appeared,
وهُوَ أُتوبيس مُكيَّف ولكِن خاص وذو طابقَيْن، فهُوَ مُميَّز جِدًّا.	12	which is air conditioned but private, and with two floors, thus it is very unique.
امممم... اااه... كما توجد أَيْضًا الميكْروباصات اااه... وهِيَ تخْتلِفُ في أحْجامِها وخُطوطِها الّتي تمْشي فيها.	13	Um... uh... Also there are the microbuses, uh... and they differ in their sizes and the routes they take...
اااه... فالبَعْضُ يسعُ لِسِتّةِ رُكّاب، والبَعْض الآخر يسع لِأَربعة عشر راكِبًا.	14	Uh... some have a capacity for six passengers, and others can carry up to fourteen passengers.
كما ظهر أَيْضًا في الإسكندرية مُنذُ عِدّةِ سنواتٍ أَيْضًا "التّوكْتوك"! وهُوَ شهيرٌ جِدًّا في الهِند.	15*	Also, a couple of years ago the "tuk-tuk" appeared in Alexandria, as well. It is very popular in India.
اااه... وأعْتقِدُ أنَّهُ تمَّ استيرادُهُ مِنَ الهِند إلى مِصر،	16	And I uh... believe they were imported from India to Egypt.

ويُستخدمُ في الأماكنِ الشعبيّةِ والأزِقّةِ الضيّقةِ جِدًّا الّتي يصعُبُ للسيّاراتِ العاديةِ أنْ تتحرّكَ داخِلَها.	17	And it is used in poor areas and on very narrow alleys, where normal vehicles find it hard to move inside.
اممم... في بعْضِ المُحافظاتِ الأُخرى يوجد "المِترو" وكما هُوَ في القاهرة ااه... وهُوَ يكونُ تحْتَ الأرْضِ.	18	Um... In some other provinces, there is the "Metro", as in Cairo, and it is underground.
ااه... كما يوجد أيْضًا ما يُطلَقُ علَيْهِ "المعْديّة" ااه... وهُوَ ما يمُرُّ... ما... عنْدَ وجودِ ترْعةٍ أوْ أيِّ مُسطّعٍ مائيٍّ.	19	Also there is what is called a "ferry" uh... which passes... which... when there is a canal or a water surface.
ااه... مِثلَ المرْكبِ الّتي يمُرُّ علَيْها الناسُ مِن شطٍّ إلى آخر، ولكِن لَيْسَ هذا وارِدًا في الإسكنْدريةِ.	20	Uh... like a boat that people get on to cross over form one side to another; however, this is not applicable in Alexandria.
اممم... عادةً عِنْدَما نُسافِرُ مِن مدينةٍ لأُخرى ااه... فأمامَنا عِدّةُ خِياراتٍ:	21	Um... usually when we travel from once city to another... we have a number of options:
ااه... هُناكَ القِطارُ، والقِطارُ في مصْر ينْقسِمُ إلى درجاتٍ... ااه... حسب سِعْرِ التّذْكرةِ.	22	Uh... there is the train, and the train in Egypt is divided into classes, uh... according to the price of the ticket.
فهُناكَ المُميّزُ... ااه... والمُكيّفُ...ااه... وهُوَ ذو جَوْدةٍ أفْضلُ مِن غَيْرِ المُكيّفِ بالطّبع. ااه... كما أنّهُ أسْرعُ.	23	There is the special... uh... and the air-conditioned one, uh... which is better than the non-air-conditioned ones in quality, of course. Uh... and it is also faster.
ااه... ولكِنّهُ ينْقسِمُ إلى درجاتٍ حسب الجَوْدةِ، ويُمْكِنُ أنْ نطْلُبُ فيهِ ومشْروباتٍ ووجباتٍ حسب الطّلبِ.	24	Uh... Anyway, it is divided into classes according to quality... and we can get some drinks and meals upon request.
ااه... هذا بالنّسْبةِ للقِطاراتِ. كما يوجد أيْضًا الـ"سوبر جيت"	25	Uh... that was for trains. There is also the "Super Jet".
ااه... وهُوَ مِثلَ الأُتوبيسِ الكبيرِ ولكِنّهُ يسْتَوْعِبُ حقائبَ أكْثر مِمّا في القِطارِ،	26	Uh... and it's like a big bus, but can take more luggage than the train.
فإذا كان لدَيْكَ حقائبُ كثيرةٌ يُمْكِنُ اسْتيعابِها في الـ"سوبر جيت" لأنّهُ أُتوبيسٌ... كالأُتوبيسِ السِّياحي الضّخْمِ.	27	So if you have a lot of luggage, it could fit in the "Super Jet" because it's a bus... it's like a huge tour bus.
ااه... تخْتلِفُ مِن مكانٍ إلى مكانٍ.	28	Uh... it differs from one destination to another.
أحْيانًا أفضّلُ القِطارَ وأحْيانًا أفضّلُ السّوبر جيت حسب المحطّاتِ الّتي سيقِفُ فيها ااه... عِنْدَ ذِهابي إلى ااه... مدينةٍ أُخرى.	29	Sometimes I prefer the train, and sometimes I prefer the Super Jet, depending on the stations they will stop at. Uh... when I go to uh... another city.
ااه... كما يوجد في السّوبر جيت أيْضًا ااه... شاشةُ عرْضٍ لأفْلامٍ، وهُوَ مُكيّفٌ أيْضًا.	30	Uh... Also, in the Super Jet there is uh... a TV screen to show movies on, and it is air-conditioned, as well.
وتوجدُ وسيلةُ مُواصلاتٍ أُخرى وهُوَ الميكْروباص مُجدّدًا ولكِن الخاصّ بالمُحافظاتِ،	31	There is another means of transportation, the microbus again, but for inter-city travel,

ولكن اااه... كثير مِن النّاس لا يُفضِّلونَهُ بِسبب اااه... سُرعتِهِ الشّديدة، ولِأنَّهُ يُصبِحُ بِذلِكَ أَكْثَرَ عُرْضَةً لِحُدوثِ الحَوَادِث.	32	but uh... a lot of people do not prefer it because of its high speed, which makes it more prone to accidents.
أمممم... كما توجدُ أيضًا العربيّات الخاصّة التّابِعة لِبعْضِ الشّرِكات الخاصّة أَوْ ما نُطلِقُ عَلَيْها الـ"ليموزين".	33	Um... there are also the private cars of some private corporations, or what we call "Limousines".
امممم... مُؤَخّرًا اااه... كُنْتُ أُسافِرُ إلى القاهِرة بالسّوبر جيت،	34	Um... recently uh... I've been traveling to Cairo by Super Jet...
ولكِنّني... اااه... أَفضِّلُ عادةً القِطار لِأَنّهُ مُريحٌ أَكْثَر مِن السّوبر جيت في جلْسَتِهِ،	35	but I usually prefer the train as its seats are more comfortable than the Super Jet,
يُمْكِنُني... في اتِّساعِهِ اااه... و... وأَعْتبِرُ أَنّ الرّحْلة بِالقِطار هِيَ رِحْلةٌ بِذاتِها...	36	and I can... and in its spaciousness. Uh... and I consider traveling by a train a journey itself...
يعْني في حدّ ذاتِها هِيَ رِحْلة ومُمْتِعة لِلغاية،	37	I mean by its very nature it's a very enjoyable journey.
ولكِن بِسببِ الأَعْطالِ الكثيرة الّتي حدّثت مُؤَخّرًا في مِصر،	38	However, due to the operational delays that happened recently in Egypt,
فكُنْتُ مُضْطرّة إلى أَنْ أَذْهبَ بِالسّوبر جيت عِوضًا عنِ القِطار.	39	I had to take the Super Jet instead of the train.
امممم... هذِهِ كانت هِيَ وسائِلُ المواصلات في الإِسْكَنْدرية ومِنَ الإِسْكَنْدرية إلى مُحافظات أُخرى.	40	Um... these were the means of transportation in Alexandria, and from Alexandria to other cities.
شُكْرًا جزيلًا.	41	Thanks a lot.

Notes

*1 Alexandria takes the definite article in MSA: الإِسْكَنْدرية, but not in the Egyptian dialect: إسكَنْدرية.

*5 In MSA, inanimate plurals are grammatically feminine singular. "Them" would be ـها. Alaa uses this correctly in line 4. However, in the Egyptian dialect, the masculine plural is commonly used even for inanimate objects. Influenced by her native dialect, Alaa says هُم instead of ـها several times in this segment, as in line 5. This is a good example of the types of mistakes that native speakers might make. Native speakers of Arabic all speak their local dialect naturally. When speaking MSA, which is learned at school, a level of attention and concentration is required to avoid mixing it with one's dialect. Alaa is certainly well aware of this particular grammatical difference between MSA and the Egyptian dialect, but very understandably slips at times, something which is inevitable in spontaneous MSA speech.

*9 I highly recommend the book *Taxi* by Khaled Al Khamissi: **wikipedia.org/wiki/Taxi_(book)**

*15 توكْتوك (plural: تكاتك), known as *tuk-tuk* or *auto-rickshaw* in English is a small three-wheeled vehicle, as pictured here. More on Wikipedia: **bit.ly/1wgsbeo**

tuk-tuk in Egypt

Focus

What is usually termed *elative* in Arabic grammar correlates to *comparative adjectives* in English. In English, the comparative is formed either by adding __-er or more __, according to the rules of English grammar. Likewise, the Arabic elative is formed in two ways. Many basic adjectives are formed using the pattern أَفْعَل. Other adjectives, including all participles of augmented (i.e. non-measure I verbs) verbs, are formed using أَكْثَر (or sometimes a synonymous word such as أَشَدّ) followed by an indefinite accusative masdar. Nisba adjectives are similarly followed by the indefinite accusative feminine form.

كَبير	big	أَكْبَر	bigger
شَيِّق	interesting	أَكْثَر تشويقًا	more interesting
مُنْصِف	fair	أَكْثَر إنْصافًا	fairer
مُهْمِل	careless	أَكْثَر إهْمالًا	more careless
مِلْحي	salty	أَكْثَر مِلْحيَّةً	saltier

The elative can also correspond to the superlative (the __-est, the most __) when definite: البَيْت الأَكْبَر *the biggest house*. It can also precede a plural (or dual) noun or pronoun suffix to mean *the __-est of the __s*: أَكْبَر البُيوتِ *the biggest of the houses*; أَكْبَرُها *the biggest (one) of them*.

Find examples of the elative in the text and write them below along with their translations. The line numbers you will find examples on are provided below.

line number	Arabic	English
4		
4		
4		
5		
5		
9		
23		
23		
26		
32		
35		

Childhood Memory

Key Words

كتْكوت chick   حمامّة pigeon   دجاجة hen   نسْر vulture; eagle

Main Idea

    a. Atheer explains a game he would play with his brothers.
    b. Atheer relates a fond memory from school.
    c. Atheer relates a funny experience from his uncle's poultry farm.
    d. Atheer relates several childhood memories.

True or False

    1. As a child, Atheer loved drinking milk.
    2. Atheer has two brothers.
    3. "Game of Geniuses" was a video game Atheer would play with his friends.
    4. Atheer rode his green bicycle to school every day.
    5. Atheer recalls a fun lesson from elementary school.

Multiple Choice

1. What did Atheer do with the milk his mom bought him?

    a. He spilled it in the car.
    b. He gave it to a beggar.
    c. He threw it away.
    d. He gulped it down.

2. Atheer thought that pigeons were ___.

    a. female roosters   b. flying rats   c. young eagles   d. funny looking

3. Atheer used to play a game with his friends which involved ___.

    a. cards with notable Arab personalities
    b. bicycle racing
    c. tasting food
    d. counting birds

4. Osama was Atheer's ___.

    a. teacher   b. father   c. brother   d. friend

5. Atheer didn't tell about ___.

    a. a time he got hurt
    b. a time he got into trouble
    c. a time he got lost
    d. any of the above

Matching

MSA	ICA	English
أتكلّم	شونْكُمْ؟	a few
أَحْيانًا	شْنو أَخْبارُكُمْ؟	a little (bit)
أعْتقِدُ	راح	a lot
الآن	أَحْچي	after
أَيْضًا	كم	also; too
بعْدَ أنْ	ساعات	bicycle
بعْض الـ	هْوايَ	How are you?
درّاجة	همّيْن	I talk
ديك	مو	I think
سَوْفَ	شْوَيّة	I was
قليلًا	چِنِت	in order to; so that
كثيرًا	وَراء ما	not
كُنْتُ	شُمر	now
كَيْفَ حالُكَ؟	أَكو	rooster
لِكَيْ	لَيْش	sometimes
لِماذا	هسّة	there is; there are
لَيْسَ	عبالي	this
ما الأخْبار؟	ديچ	throw away
نبذَ، ألْقى	روحك	What's up?
نفْسُكَ	هايْ	why
هذهِ، تِلْكَ	على مَوْد	will
يوجد	بايْسِكْل	yourself
ثُمَّ	ويّا	like that
ذلِكَ	سوّى	that
شَيْء	هيجي	then; after that
فعلَ	شِيء	thing
مَعَ	ووَراءها	to do
هكذا، كذلِكَ	ذاك	with

Answers

Main Idea: d **True or False:** 1. F[4] 2. T[11] 3. F[14] 4. F[20-21] 5. T[22-24] **Multiple Choice:** 1. c[6] 2. c[9] 3. a[14] 4. d[17] 5. d

Matching: شوْنكُم؟ How are you? / كَيْفَ حالَكَ؟ / ما الأخْبار / راح will / سَوْفَ / What's up? شنو أخْبارِكُم؟ / أتكلّم I talk / أحْكي / كم a few

/ كِنت I was / قليلًا a little (bit) / شوَيَّة / مو not لَيَسَ / أيْضًا / also; too همَّيْن / كثيرًا / a lot هُوايَ / أحْيانًا sometimes ساعات / بعْض الـ

/ عبالي I think / الآن now هسّة / لِماذا why لَيْش / يوجد there is; there are / نبذ، ألقى throw away شُمَر / بعْدَ أنْ after كُنْتُوَراء ما

ويّا / دِرّاجة bicycle بايْسِكَل / لِكَيْ in order to; so that على مَوْد / هذِه، تِلْكَ this هايْ / نفْسُكَ yourself روحك / ديك rooster ديچ / أعْتقِدُ

with مَعَ / سِوى to do سوّى / فعَلَ / like that هيجي / هكذا، كذلَكَ / شيء thing شَيْء / ووَراءها / then; after that ثُمَّ / ذاك that ذلِكَ

Text

شوْنكُم؟ شْنو أخْبارِكُم؟	**1**	How are you? What's up?
اليَوْم راح أحْكي عن كم شغْلة صارت بِطُفولْتي،	**2***	Today I'm going to talk about a few things that happened in my childhood.
يعْني هِيَ عِبارة عن ذِكْرَيات ساعات الواحِد مَن يتْذكّرُها يضْحك ويضْحك هُوايَ همَّيْن، مو شْوَيَّة.	**3**	That is, they are memories that, when one recalls them, he laughs and laughs a lot, too, not a little.
المُهِمّ وحْدة مِن الشغْلات أتْذكّر چِنت أنا وأُمّي رايْحين لِلسّوق وأنا أدْري بروحي ما أُحِبّ الحليب.	**4***	Anyway, one of the things I remember is my mom and I were going to the market, and I know that I don't like milk,
شُفْت محلّ يبيع عُلب حليب كارْتون ولحَّيْت على أُمّي إلّا تِشْتريلي مِنَه.	**5**	[but] I saw a shop that sells milk [in] cartons. And I pestered my mom, [saying] "Won't you buy me one?"
ووَراء ما اشْترتْلي رأسًا شِرْبْت مِنَه شْوَيّة وشُمرْته.	**6**	After she bought [some] for me, straight away I drank a little bit of it, and threw it away.
حتّى أذْكر چان أكو ناس قالوا لَيْش شُمرْته؟	**7**	I even remember there were people saying, "Why did you throw it away?"
وحْدة مِن الشغْلات اِلْي كُلّ ما أذكُرها هسّة أضْحك هْوايَّ	**8**	One of the things that, every time I recall now, I laugh a lot
وهِيَ إنّهُ چِنت عبالي الكتْكوت الصّغيِّر ااه... من يكْبر شْوَيّة يصير حمامّة ووَراءها دجاجة ووَراءها ديچ وبعْدَيْن نسْر.	**9**	is that I used to think that little chicks grow to become pigeons, and then chickens, and then roosters, and, after that, eagles.
ومرّة همَّيْن أذْكُر بالمدْرسة لمّا كانوا يسْألون: كم أخو عنْدك؟	**10**	Another time I remember at school is when they would ask, "How many brothers and sisters do you have?"
كِنْت أقول إحْنا ثلاثة مع العِلْم أنا عنْدي أخْوان اِثْنَيْن بسّ.	**11**	I'd say "There are three of us," knowing that I just had two brothers.
وچِنت أحْسب روحي همَّيْن لِحدّ ما أُمّي قالتْلي: شنو؟ أنْتَ أخو روحك يعْني؟	**12**	I'd count myself, too, until my mother asked me, "What? Are you your own brother, too?"
مِن الشغْلات اِلْي أذكُر چِنّا نِتْونّس بها نِسوّيها أنا وأصْدِقائي إنّهُ نِلْعب لُعْبة اِسْمها لُعْبة الأذْكِياء	**13**	Something I recall that my friends and I used to enjoy and do is that we'd play a game called "Game of Geniuses",

وهِيَ عِبارة عن لُعْبة ورق، بسّ كُلّ كارْت مكْتوب علَيْه شخْصية عربية مُعيّنة سَواء بالتّاريخ أوْ بالعِلْم أوْ بالأدب وغَيْرَه.	14	which was a card game, but every card had, written on it, a certain Arab personality from history or science or literature, etc.
وأذكُر هايْ اللّعْبة چِنّا ساعات نِتْعارك علَيْها على مود نِفوز.	15	And I remember we'd sometimes battle it out to win at that game.
مِن الأشْياء اِلّي چِنت أحِبّها بِطُفولْتي أيْضًا هِيَ البايْسِكْلات.	16	One of the things I really loved in my childhood was bicycles.
چان عِنْدي بايْسِكل أخْضر حِجْم سِتّة عش إنْچ وكِنت دايْمًا أفْترّ علَيْه أنا وصديقي أُسامة،	17	I had a green, sixteen-inch bicycle that me and my friend Osama would go around on.
وساعات أخُذ أخوي ويّاي لِحدّ ما أبْوي جابْله بايْسِكل	18	And sometimes I'd take my brother with me until my dad got him a bicycle.
ووَراءْها ما بقى يطلُب البايْسِكل مالْتي.	19	And after that, he didn't request [to borrow] my bicycle [anymore].
چِنت أتْمَنّى أقْدر أروح لِلْمدْرسة بالبايْسِكل	20	I was hoping to be able to go to school by bike,
بسّ چان ممْنوع نِسوّي هيچي لِإنّ بُيوتْنا چانت بعيدة شْوَيّة عن المدْرسة وما يِقْبلون لإنّ يِخافون علَيْنا.	21	but we weren't allowed to do that because our house was a bit far from school and they wouldn't accept it because they were worried about us.
وآخِر شي أتْذكّره إنّه بالاِبْتِدائية المُعلِّمة مالة العُلوم سوّتلْنا تجْرُبة لِحاسّة الذّوق	22	The final thing I remember is in elementary school the science teacher had us do an experiment for the sense of taste.
وجِبْنا كُلّنا أكل وغمضت عُيونْنا ووَراءْها بدَيْنا نِتْذوّق الأكل وأذكُر چان اِسْم المُعلِّمة آمنة	23	She brought all of us food and closed our eyes, and then we started to taste the food. I remember the teacher's name was Amina.
وچان درْس العُلوم كُلّش مُمْتِع ذاك الوَقْت.	24	It was a really interesting science lesson that day.

Notes

*2 The letter چ is used to represent the sound [tʃ], as in the *ch* in the English word *chat,* a sound represent in the Iraqi dialect which replaces ك [k] in many cases.

*4 The particle ما is used to make both the present and past tenses negative. (MSA: لا and لم, respectively).

Clothing in Morocco

Key Words

أَلْبِسة clothing	يَنْتمي إلى belongs to
لِباس wearing	يَرْتدي wears

Main Idea

a. Western-style dress is largely rejected by Moroccans.
b. Most men wear the djellaba and fez.
c. Nowadays, most people in Morocco dress like Westerners.
d. Men generally wear Western-style clothing, while women continue to dress traditionally.

True or False

1. In Casablanca, only the wealthy wear jeans.
2. In Morocco, the type of clothes differ from region to region.
3. Both men and women wear djellabas.
4. Most men still wear the djellaba and fez.
5. Traditional Moroccan clothes are nowadays only worn on special occasions.

Multiple Choice

1. Trends in clothing differ by ___.

    a. age group   c. geographic location
    b. social class d. *all of the above*

2. Which is **not** true?

    a. Southerners wear the dira'ah.
    b. Northerners wear the milhaf.
    c. Easterners wear the wajdiyah.
    d. Mountain people wear the qishabah.

3. Which two of the following does Abdelhak mention about Moroccan women?

    a. They rarely wear jeans.
    b. They dress less modestly than in the past.
    c. They embroider djellabas.
    d. They usually wear the hijab.

4. What is mentioned as a reason for the diminishment in the importance of the traditional Moroccan dress?

    a. urbanization   c. secularization
    b. globalization   d. poverty

5. Moroccan youth follow the latest ___ fads.

   a. European, American, and Asian
   b. European, American, and Egyptian
   c. American, Egyptian, and Lebanese
   d. Egyptian, Lebanese, and Tunisian

Matching

حسبَ	according to
حتّى	as well as
سَواءً... أوْ	because of
هُناكَ	even
كما أنَّ	is considered
يُعْتَبَرُ	overall, generally
ما يُسمّى بِ	than previously, than in the past
عُمومًا	there is, there are
وكذلِكَ بِسببِ	what is called
مِنَ السّابِق	whether... or

Answers

Main Idea: c **True or False:** 1. F 2. T 3. T 4. F 5. T **Multiple Choice:** 1. d 2. b 3. b & c 4. b 5. a **Matching:** حسبَ according to / حتّى even / سَواءً... أوْ whether... or / هُناكَ there is, there are / كما أنَّ as well as / يُعْتَبَرُ is considered / ما يُسمّى بِ what is called / عُمومًا overall, generally / وكذلِكَ بِسببِ because of / مِنَ السّابِق than previously, than in the past

Text

تخْتلِفُ أنْماطُ الألْبِسةِ في المغْرِب حسبَ الفِئاتِ العُمْرية والطّبقاتِ الاِجْتِماعية وحتّى المَواقِع الجُغْرافية.	1	Trends in clothing in Morocco differ according to age group, social class, and even geographical location.
ففي المُدُنِ الكُبْرى كمدينة الدّار البَيْضاء حَيْثُ يُلاحَظ اِنْفِتاح الشّباب على... الغرْب وتأثُّرِهِم بِلِباسِهِم	2	In big cities like Casablanca, the openness of youth toward the West and its effects on what they wear can be observed,
حَيْثُ جينْز يطْغى على ذَوْقِ العامّة، سَواءً الأغْنِياء أوْ الفُقَراء.	3	where jeans dominate the tastes of the populace, be they rich or poor.
وهُناكَ نَوْع مِنَ التّحرُّر في اللِّباس بِالنِّسْبةِ لِلْعُنْصِر النِسْوي،	4	Uh, there is a kind of liberalization in the dress of the female populace,

كما أنَّ شكْلَ اللِّباسِ يخْتلِفُ مِن مِنْطقة إلى أُخْرى.	5	as well as the type of clothes differing from region to region,
وهُوَ رمْزٌ تُراثِي وثقافِي يُعْتبَرُ كصُورة تُمثِّلُ المِنْطقةَ الّتي ينْتمِي إلَيْها الفرْد.	6	which is a symbol of heritage and culture that is considered an illustration of the region the individual belongs to.
ممم... فمثلًا اللِّباسُ في الجنُوب مُميَّزٌ عن غَيْرِهِ في الشَّمال،	7	For example, clothing in the south is distinct from that in the north,
فأهْلُ الجنُوب يرْتدونَ ما يُسمّى بالدّراعِيَة والمِلْحاف	8	as southerners wear what is called dira'ah or milhaf.
وسُكّانُ الشّرْق يرْتدونَ ما يُسمّى بالوَجْدِيَة	9	And people in the east wear what is called wajdiyah.
وسُكّانُ الجبال يرْتدونَ ما يُسمّى بالقشابة.	10	And mountain people wear what is called qishabah.
وعُمومًا فاللِّباسُ في المغْرِب مُميَّزٌ جِدًّا.	11	Overall, clothing is quite distinctive in Morocco.
فالمرْأةُ تتفنّنُ في حِياكة وخِياطة وطرْزِ أحْسنِ أنْواعِ القفاطِين والجلابِيب	12	Women excel at weaving, tailoring and embroidering the best kinds of caftans and djellabas.
والرِّجالُ كذلك يرْتدونَ الجلابِيب البَيْضاء والطَّرابِيش الحمْراء والبلْغة الصّفْراء.	13	Men also wear white djellabas (robes) and the red fez and yellow babouches (slippers).
إنَّ اللِّباس المغْرِبي يُعْتبَرُ لَوْحةً غنيةً بِمُخْتلفِ الكُنوزِ الحضارِية والتّقْليدِية الّتي تزْخرُ بها الثقافة العربِية.	14	Moroccan clothing is considered a rich portrait of the various treasures of culture and tradition that Arab culture abounds in.
مُؤخّرًا قلْت أهمِّية للِّباس التّقْليدِي المغْرِبي خُصوصًا في صُفوف الشّباب	15	In recent times, the importance of traditional Moroccan dress has diminished, especially among young people,
وكذلك بِسبب العَوْلمة الّتي سهّلتِ الحُصولَ على الملابِس مِن مُخْتلف بِقاع العالم.	16	because of globalization, which has made it easy to get clothes from all over the world.
همم... فأقْبلَ الشّبابُ على ارْتداء الألْبِسة الّتي تنْتمِي إلى الثّقافة الغرْبِية.	17	Hmm... young people have turned to wearing clothes which belong to Western culture.
فأصبحوا يُتّبِعون آخِرَ الصّيْحاتِ الأُورُبِّية والأمْريكية والآسِيَوِية،	18	They've started to follow the latest European, American and Asian fads,
كما أصبحوا يُقلِّدونَ نُجوم السّينما الغرْبِية في اللِّباس.	19	as well as imitate how Western movie stars dress.
لقد تغيّرت طريقةٌ ونمط اللِّباس لدى المَغارِبة،	20	The way and style of dressing among Moroccans has changed;
فالرِّجال لم تعُدّ تسْتهْوِيهم الجلابِيب والطّرابِيش،	21	the djellaba and fez no longer appeal to men,
بل أصبحوا يُقْبِلونَ على ارْتداء السّراوِيل والأقْمِصة الرِّياضية.	22	rather they've turned to wearing pants and T-shirts.
وكذلك النِّساء أصبحْنَ يرْتدينَ ثِيابًا أقلّ حِشْمةً مِنَ السّابق.	23	Likewise, women have begun to dress less modestly than previously.
وأصبحتِ الملابِسُ المغْرِبية الأصِيلة تُلْبَسُ فقط في المُناسِبات.	24	Native Moroccan clothes have come to be worn only on special occasions.

Focus

أَصْبَحَ followed by an accusative noun means *become:* أَصْبَحَ طَبِيبًا *He became a doctor.* However, when followed by an indicative verb, it could translate as *begin to* or *come to,* showing a change: أَصْبَحْتُ أَفْهَمُ *I came to understand.*

Translate the following phrases using the verbs provided. Then check your answers in the text.

تَبِعَ *to follow*		they've started to follow
قَلَّدَ *to imitate*		they've begun to imitate
أَقْبَلَ على إِرْتِداء *to turn to wearing*		they've turned to wearing
اِرْتَدى *to wear*		women have begun to wear
لُبِسَ *to be worn*		Native Moroccan clothes have come to be worn

Technology

Key Words

التّكْنولوجِيا	technology	أَجْهِزة	devices
موباﻳْل	cell phone	تحْميل	downloading

Main Idea

   a.   The Internet has improved communication between individuals.
   b.   Technology has both positive and negative consequences in our lives.
   c.   Pirating movies, music, and books is widespread problem.
   d.   Many people are addicted to the Internet and their smart phones.

True or False

   1.   Arab society isn't as dependent on technology as the West.
   2.   Technology has damaged relationships within families.
   3.   People waste too much time on the Internet.
   4.   Technology can save people a lot of time.
   5.   Engy sometimes wishes she didn't have a smart phone.

Multiple Choice

   1.   Engy says, at family gatherings, you often see ___ engaging in conversation with others.

          a.   only younger family members   c.   only older family members
          b.   most family members   d.   all family members

   2.   Parents may encourage their children to do well at school ___.

          a.   by threatening to take away their cell phones
          b.   with the promise of getting them a new laptop
          c.   making them do their homework before they can use the Internet
          d.   downloading e-books for them

   3.   Engy mentions that people download pirated material from the Internet because ___ and ___.

          a.   laws protecting intellectual property are not enforced
          b.   it saves them time
          c.   it saves them money
          d.   they often cannot find legitimate copies for sale online.

   4.   Engy mentions that playing on sites such as Facebook and Twitter can be ___ and ___.

          a.   relaxing and fun   c.   harmful and wrong
          b.   a good way to keep in touch with friends   d.   a waste of time

5. Communication programs and mobile apps ___.
   a.   have allowed students to cheat on tests
   b.   have made international calls much cheaper
   c.   have allowed parents to keep track of their children better
   d.   *all of the above*

Matching

MSA	ECA	English
أصْبَحَ	بقى	And another thing is...
إلخ	محدِش يِقْدر	etc.
بِدونَ	لُه	everything
الّذي، الّتي	مِن غَيْرِ	for free
في نظري	كُلّ حاجة	has become; has come to...
كُلّ شَيْء	مِش	he has; it has
لا يُمْكِنُ لِأحد أنْ	وحاجة تانْية كمان هَيَّ إنّ	in my opinion
لا يوجد	عشان	in order to; so that...
لِكَيْ	وكِده	no one can
لَهُ	بِلاش	not
لَيْسَ	ما فيش	that; which; who
مجانًا	فيه	there isn't; there aren't
وشَيْءٌ آخر،	اِللي	there's; there are
يوجد	أنا شايْفة إنّ	without

Answers

Main Idea: x **True or False:** 1. F[3-4] 2. T[8] 3. T[20,25] 4. T[27] 5. F **Multiple Choice:** 1. c[10] 2. b[12] 3. a[18] & c[17] 4. c[26] & d[24-25] 5. b[30] **Matching:** بقى has become; has come to... أصْبَحَ / محدِش يِقْدر no one can لا يُمْكِنُ لِأحد أنْ / لُه he has; it has مِن / وشَيْءٌ آخر، / عشان in And another thing is... وحاجة تانْية كمان هَيَّ إنّ / مِش not لَيْسَ / كُلّ شَيْء everything كُلّ حاجة / بِدونَ without غَيْرِ order to; so that... لِكَيْ / وكِده etc. إلخ بِلاش for free مجانًا / ما فيش there isn't; there aren't لا يوجد / فيه there's; there are في نظري in my opinion أنا شايْفة إنّ / الّذي، الّتي that; which; who اِللي / يوجد

Text

العالَم كُلُّه حاليًا بقى مُعتمَد على التِّكْنولوجيا،	1	The entire world has become dependent on technology,
يعني ما بِيْنفَعْش نِتْخيِّل حَياتْنا مِن غَيْر الكُمْبيُوتر والإنْترْنت والموبايْل.	2*	that is, it's useless to try to imagine life without computers, the Internet and cell phones.
بالرّغْم من إنّ التِّكْنولوجيا دي انْتشرت في العالم العربي في أوَاخِر التِّسْعينيات أوَائِل الألْفَيْنيات	3	Although this technology only spread through the Arab world in the late nineties and early two-thousands,
إلّا أنّها أصبحت لها مكانة كْبيرة جِدًّا، لِدرجة إنّ محدِش بِيْقدر بِتْخيِّل الحياة مِن غَيْرها.	4	it has assumed such large place that no one can imagine life without it.
لكن زَيّ ما كُلّ حاجة لها سلْبياتْها وإيجابياتْها، كمان مَوْضوع التِّكْنولوجيا ده لُه مُميِّزاتُه وعُيوبُه.	5	But just as everything has negatives and positives, also technology has advantages and disadvantages.
فمثلًا بالرّغْم من إنّ الموبايْل والإنْترْنت بقوا بِيْوصّلوا بَيْن النّاس بِطريقة أسْرع وأسْهل	6*	For example, although cell phones and the Internet have come to connect people faster and more easily,
لكن إحْنا مُجتمعْنا بِيْعاني مِن بُرود وبُعد العلاقات بَيْن أفْرادُه.	7	we as a society suffer from insensitivity and deteriorations in relationships between its members.
ومِش حَأكون بِبالِغ لَوْ قُلْتَ إنّ البُرود ده بقى بَين أفْراد الأُسْرة الواحْدة،	8	And I wouldn't be going too far to say that this insensitivity exists between members of a family.
حتّى إنُّه مُمْكِن تِكون أُسْرة كْبيرة مِتْجمّعة وأغْلب أفْرادْها خاصّةً الشّباب بِيْكونوا مشْغولين في تِليفونْهُم أوْ في الآيْباد أوْ التّابْليت أوْ غَيْرها مِن الأجْهِزة الحديثة.	9	It's even possible that a large family can be gathered together and most of the family members, especially the younger people, are busy with their phones, iPads, tablets, or other modern devices.
محدِش بِيْندمج في الأحاديث الأُسْرية غَيْر الأفْراد الأكْبر سِنًّا.	10	No one's partaking in family conversations except the older members.
وحاجة تانْية كمان هَيّ إنّ مَوْضوع التِّكْنولوجيا بالنِّسْبة لِبعض أفْراد المُجتمع وخاصّةً الشّباب بقى غاية ومِش وسيلة.	11	And another thing is that technology, for some members of society and especially for young people, has been an ends rather than a means.
يعني مثلًا الحافِز أوْ الحاجة اللي الأهْل بِيْشجِّعوا بها ولادْهُم عشان يِذاكِروا وينْجحوا في تعْليمْهُم بِتْكون موبايْل جديد أوْ لاب توب جديد.	12	That is, for example, the motivation or the thing that the family encourages their children with so they'll study and succeed at school is a new cell phone or new laptop.
لأ، وكمان مُمْكِن حد يِحوِّش مصْروفُه لِفترات طَويلة عشان يِشْتري موبايْل جديد أوْ يِغيِّر تِليفونُه القديم، وكِده.	13	No, and it's also possible that someone save up for a long time to buy a new cell phone or change his old phone, etc.
وِللأسف، اتْغيِّرت عادات كِثير في مُجتمعْنا بِسبب التِّكْنولوجيا الحديثة.	14	Sadly, customs have changed a lot in our society because of modern technology.
يعني مثلًا محدِش بقى بِيِشْتري كُتُب. كُلّ النّاس بِتْقرأ النُّسَخ الإلِكْترونية مِن الكُتُب.	15	For example, no one buys books. Everyone reads electronic copies of books.

وكده برضُه فيه الأفْلام والأغاني.	16	And there are movies and songs, too.
النُّسَخ المُهرَّبة مَوْجودة على الإنْترنت ودي الحاجة اِلْلي بِتْخلّي النّاس تِوفَّر أسْعار تذاكِر السينما وتِتْفرّج على الإنْترنت بِبلاش.	17	Pirated copies are found on the Internet, and this is something that has allowed people to save money on movie tickets and watch them on the Internet for free.
وِده طبْعًا لِأنّ ما فيش قَوانين بِتْنظّم المَوْضوع ده.	18	And this, of course, is because there aren't any laws regulating this matter.
وِقَوانين حِماية المِلْكية الفِكْرية مِش مُفعّلة ولّا واضْحة.	19	Laws protecting intellectual property are neither enforced nor clear.
وِمِن أكْبر عُيوب التكْنولوجيا مِن وِجْهة نظري هيَّ تضْييع الوقْت لِأنّ الأفْراد في مُجْتمعي بِيسْتخْدِموا الإنْترنت وأجْهِزة الحديثة بِطريقة تِضيّع الوقْت بِشكْلَ كْبير جِدًّا.	20	One of the biggest shames of technology, in my opinion, is its waste of time, because people in my community use the Internet and modern devices in a way that is very wasteful of time.
وِمِش بِيحقّقوا أيّ فايْدة بِالرّغْمَ مِن الوقْت الطّويل اِلْلي بْيِضيّعوه في اِسْتِخْدام التكْنولوجيا دي،	21	They're not doing anything useful in spite of all the time they're wasting using this technology,
زيّ مثلًا إنّ فيه ناس بِتْضيّع وقْتَ كْبير في عمل نغمات أوْ رنّات لِلتِّليفون.	22	as, for example, there are people who waste a lot of time making melodies or ring tones for the telephone.
وِفيه ناس بِتْضيّع وقْتَها في تحْميل ولِعْب الألْعاب.	23	There are people who waste time downloading and playing games.
وِفيه ناس بِيسْتخْدِموا مَواقِع التَّواصُل الاِجْتِماعي فَيْسْبوك وتِوِيتِر وِغَيْرها في الهِزار والنُّكت	24	And there are people who use the social networking sites Facebook and Twitter and others for fooling around and playing,
وِمِن غَيْر ما يحقّقوا أيّ فايْدة لِساعات طَويلة جِدًّا مِن اليَوْم.	25	but without producing any benefits and for hours and hours of the day.
وِكُلّ دي اِسْتِخْدامات غلط وِمُضرّة. لكِن برضُه لِلتّكنولوجيا مُميّزاتها.	26	All of these uses are wrong and harmful. But technology also has its merits.
طبْعًا وُجود التكْنولوجيا بِيْوفّر جِدًّا في الوقْت.	27	Of course, the existence of technology saves a lot of time.
يعْني خِدْمة بسيطة بِنْلاقيها على شبكة الإنْترنت زمان كانت بِتاخُذ وقْتَ طَويل جِدًّا، زَيّ مثلًا البحْث عن العناوين اِلْلي بقى سهْل جِدًّا بِسبب الخرائِط الإلكْترونية.	28	That is, basic services we can find on the Internet used to take a lot of time, like, for example, looking up addresses, which has become really easy because of electronic maps.
وبرامج الاِتّصالات وتطْبيقات الموبايْل اِلْلي بِتْسهِّل الاِتِّصال، اِلْلي كان مِن المَوْضوعات المُكلِّفة جِدًّا.	29	Communication programs and mobile apps that facilitate communication, which used to be quite costly,
فكان الناس اِلْلي بِيتْكلّموا دُوَلي بِيتْكلّموا مُكالمات عالية التّكاليف. وكانِت بِتِبْقى المُكالمات سريعة جِدًّا وعلى فترات مُتباعْدة، لكِن حاليًا المَوْضوع بقى أرْخص وأسْهل.	30	as people who made international calls, so they'd make them quick and infrequently, but now it's become cheaper and faster.

فَأَنا شايْفة إنّ التكْنولوجِيا الحديثة زَيّها زَيّ أَيّ حاجة تانْية في الدُّنْيا،	**31**	So from my point of view, I view technology as anything else in the world:
أَضْرارها وفَوايِدْها بِتِعْتِمد على الطّريقة اِلْلي بِنِسْتخْدِمْها بِها.	**32**	its disadvantages and its advantages depend on the way we use them.

Notes

*2 The negative is formed by sandwiching a verb (or particle) with ما...ش.

*6 Egypt Arabic, as many other dialects of Arabic, adds the prefix بِ *bi-* to mark the present tense. The 3rd person plural suffix is ـوا *-ū* (MSA: ـونَ)

Cats and Dogs

Key Words

قِطَّة (قِطط) cat	حَيَوان أليف pet	تَرْبِيَة raising
كَلْب (كِلاب) dog	ضالّ stray	

Main Idea

a. Cats and dogs are popular pets in Egypt.
b. Hend explains attitudes in Egypt toward pets and strays.
c. Hend explains why cats are more popular than dogs in Egypt.
d. Cats and dogs were revered and sacred in Ancient Egypt.

True or False

1. Dogs are more popular among working class people than among the affluent.
2. Pets are **not** allowed in most apartments in Egypt.
3. Hend feels that stray cats are better off than stray dogs in Egypt.
4. Animal shelters are rare in Egypt.
5. Hend mentions that the humane treatment of strays is an Islamic principle.

Multiple Choice

1. What does Hend say about dogs living inside the house?

    a. Most people's apartments are too small for dogs.
    b. Most people's rental agreements do not allow them to keep dogs.
    c. Islamic culture frowns on keeping dogs inside the house.
    d. In Egyptian culture, keeping dogs inside the house is very popular.

2. Which of the following two are true?

    a. Dogs are preferred among the upper class.
    b. Cats are preferred among the upper class.
    c. Dogs are more popular than cats among the middle class.
    d. Cats are more popular than dogs among the middle class.

3. Egyptian society is not overly concerned with animal welfare because ___.

    a. it is not an Islamic value
    b. the country is still struggling for human rights
    c. they are seen as a source of danger and annoyance
    d. *all of the above*

4. The government has a program to ___.

    a. neuter stray dogs and cats   c. place strays in animal shelters
    b. kill strays with poisoned meat   d. throw strays into the sea

5. As a well-known Islamic story goes, ___.

    a. a woman who kept pets in her house went to hell
    b. a woman kind to animals went to paradise, while a woman cruel to animals went to hell
    c. a woman kind to cats went to paradise, while a woman kind to dogs went to hell
    d. a woman who poisoned strays with meat went to hell

Matching

بَيْنما	as for; when it comes to
غالِبًا ما	because (of)
أمّا بِالنِّسْبةِ لِ	better off than
ما زالت	either... or...
في أغْلبِ الأحْوال	endless
أفْضلُ حالًا مِنَ	in most cases
أكْثرَ قُدْرةً على	more capable of
سَواءً... أوْ...	namely
نظرًا لِ	no doubt; certainly
ألا وهُوَ	still
على اسْتِحْياء	tentatively
لا نِهايةَ لهُ	usually
بِالتّأْكيد	while; on the other hand

Answers

Main Idea: b **True or False:** 1. F[2] 2. F[8] 3. T[11-12] 4. T[16] 5. T[20-21] **Multiple Choice:** 1. c[4] 2. a[2] & d[5-6] 3. b[10] 4. b[16-17] 5. b[22-24] **Matching:** بَيْنما while; on the other hand / غالِبًا ما usually / أمّا بِالنِّسْبةِ لِ as for; when it comes to / ما زالت still / نظرًا لِ either... or... / سَواءً... أوْ... / أكْثرَ قُدْرةً على more capable of / أفْضلُ حالًا مِنَ better off than / في أغْلبِ الأحْوال in most cases / بِالتّأْكيد no doubt; certainly / لا نِهايةَ لهُ endless / على اسْتِحْياء tentatively / ألا وهُوَ namely / because (of)

Text

يَرْتَبِطُ اقْتِناءُ القِطَطِ والكِلابِ الأليفة في مِصر بالطّبقة الاجْتماعية الّتي تَمْلِكُ رفاهية العِنايةِ بها.	1	Having cats and dogs as pets in Egypt is restricted to a sector of the society that has the luxury of affording to care for them.
فتشيعُ تربيةُ الكِلابِ مثلًا في وسط المُوسِرين الّذين يَمْلِكونَ منازِلَ كبيرةً مُزوّدةً بحدائق.	2	Dogs are, for example, preferred among the affluent who have big houses with gardens.
بَيْنما يتجنّبُها مُعْظم من يعيشونَ في شُقق سكنية	3	On the other hand, they are avoided by most of those who live in apartments
حَيْثُ إنَّ الدّينَ الإسلامي لا يُحبّدُ تربيَةَ الكِلابِ في داخلِ البُيُوت.	4	because the Islamic culture doesn't recommend raising dogs inside the house.
بالنّسبةِ للقطط الأليفة فهِيَ أكْثَرُ انْتِشارًا مِنَ الكِلاب	5	As for pet cats, they are more prevalent than dogs,
حَيْثُ يقْتنيها مُحبّو الحَيَوَانات مِنَ الطّبقتَيْن الموسرة والمُتَوَسِّطة.	6	as animal lovers from both the high and middle classes might have them.
غالبًا ما يهْتمُّ مُحبّو الحَيَوَانات الأليفة بحَيَوَاناتِهم ويُحرِصونَ على نظافتِها وتطْعيمِها.	7	Pet lovers usually care for their animals and make sure they are clean and vaccinated.
ولا يوجدُ ما يَمْنعُ بشكلٍ رسمي تربِيَةَ القِطَطِ أوْ حتّى الكِلاب في داخِلِ البُيوت.	8	It is uncommon to have a legal agreement that states that cats, or even dogs, are not allowed in an apartment.
أمّا بالنّسبةِ للقِطَطِ والكِلابِ الضّالّة في مِصر فهِيَ لَيْست بأوْفر حظًّا مِنَ البشر.	9	On the other hand, when it comes to stray cats and dogs in Egypt, they are not any luckier than humans.
في دَوْلةٍ ما زالت تخوضُ معْركةَ حُقوقِ الإنْسان ويرْفُلُ فيها البشر تحْتَ عبءِ الضُّغوطِ الماديةِ والسِّياسية، يُصْبحُ الحديثُ عن حقوقِ القِطَطِ والكِلابِ الضّالّة مذعاةً للسُّخْريةِ في أغْلَبِ الأحْوال.	10	In a country still struggling for human rights, and where people suffer under the burdens of financial and political pressures, talking about the rights of stray cats and dogs ends up as material for sarcasm in most cases.
وإنْ كانتِ القِطَطُ أفْضَلُ حالًا مِنَ الكِلاب،	11	However, cats seem to be better-off than dogs.
فطبيعتُها تجعلُها أكْثَرَ قُدْرةً على التأقْلُم مع الظُروفِ القاسية لحياةِ الشّوَارع،	12	Their nature makes them more capable of coping with the tough circumstances of street life,
بَيْنما تعْتبرُ الكِلابُ الضّالّة مصْدرًا للخطرِ والإزعاج.	13	while dogs are usually seen as sources of danger and annoyance.
فحينَ تتكاثرُ في المناطقِ المأْهولةِ بالسُّكّان يخْشى النّاس أن تُؤذِّيَهُم سَواءً بالعَض أوْ بنشرِ الأمْراض.	14	When they multiply in inhabited areas, people fear that they might harm them either by biting or by spreading diseases.
كما ينْزعِجونَ مِن وصلاتِ النّباحِ اللّيلية.	15	They also get annoyed by their barking at night.
ونظرًا لنُدْرةِ ملاجِئ الحَيَوَانات الضّالّة في مِصر، تلْجأُ الحُكومةُ إلى ما أراهُ إجراءً قاسيًا وغَيْرَ إنْسانيّ،	16	And because stray animal shelters are rare in Egypt, the government resorts to what I find to be a cruel, inhumane procedure,
ألا وهُوَ قتْلَ تِلكَ الكِلابِ عن طريقِ اللُّحومِ المسمومة أوْ القنْصِ بالبنادِق.	17	namely killing those dogs either with poisoned meat or with guns.

على اسْتِحْياء تبْرُزُ بعْضُ المنظماتِ الأهْلية للرّفْق بالحَيَوَان فتقومُ بإنْقاذِ القططِ والكلابِ الضّالّة وإيوَائها في ملاجِئَ يُموِّلُها مُحِبّو الحَيَوَانات مِنَ الموسِرين.	18	Tentatively, a few animal rights' non-governmental organizations rescue stray cats and dogs and place them in animal shelters funded by well-to-do animal lovers.
ولكِن تبْقى تِلْكَ الجُهودُ نُقْطةً في بحْرٍ لا نِهايةَ له.	19	However, all these efforts remain nothing but a drop of water in an endless ocean.
بالتّأكيد تحْتاجُ القططُ والكِلابُ الضّالةُ إلى المزيدِ مِنَ الرحْمةِ والإنْسانية	20	No doubt, stray cats and dogs need more merciful, humane treatment,
الّتي تحُضُّ علَيْها أبْسطُ تعاليم الإسْلام،.	21	which is among the most fundamental Islamic principles.
الّتي ترْوِي أنَّ امرأةً سقت كلْبًا	22	A [well-known Islamic] story is that of a woman who offered water to a [thirsty] dog
فكانَ جزاؤُها الجنّة،	23	and she was granted [a place in] paradise,
بَيْنما أخْرى حبست قِطّةً فمنعت عنْها الطّعام فكانَ عِقابُها هُوَ الجحيم.	24	while another neglected feeding a cat that she owned and her punishment was hell.

Focus

Review the rules for elatives in the Focus for segment 15. Then find and examine examples of elatives in *this* segment. (Examples can be found in lines 5, 9, 10, 11, and 12.)

Religion

Key Words

مسيحي Christian	صِيام fasting
طائِفة (طَّوائِف) sect	جيل generation

Main Idea

a. Luma explains how the "Western Religion", Christianity, has led to social decay in Jordan.

b. Luma explains the harmonious situation in Lebanon between Christianity and Islam and also the moral character among the young generation.

c. Luma describes the tumultuous relationship between Christians and Muslims in Jordan and the frequent sectarian conflicts her country experiences.

d. Luma compares the older and younger generations' attitudes toward religion.

True or False

1. There is a great deal of conflict and animosity between Muslims and Christians in Jordan.
2. Luma doesn't know many details about Christian sects in Jordan.
3. The majority Muslim sect in Jordan is Sunni; Shi'as make up a small minority.
4. Luma mentions that some young Jordanians are very Westernized.
5. Luma believes that religion and ethics are two entirely separate things.

Multiple Choice

1. Luma tells us that Christians ___ in Jordan.

   a. have religious freedom
   b. must worship in secret
   c. live in separate communities
   d. make up less than 20% of the population

2. During Ramadan, Christians ___

   a. fast alongside Muslims
   b. disregard any festivities
   c. refrain from eating in public out of respect
   d. have their own festivities and rituals

3. Luma says than many young people are civilized and respectful, ___.

   a. and they are dedicated to their religion, rejecting all Western culture
   b. but they heedlessly take bad customs from the West and America just to be "cool"
   c. and they only adopt from the West what is in line with their religion and culture
   d. but they have been led astray by religious extremism

4. Luma says that some young people ___.

   a. are heedless and uninterested in morals
   b. adopt Western customs that do not conform to local values
   c. complain that the Arab world does not understand them
   d. *all of the above*

5. Luma herself is ____.

    a. Sunni   b. Shi'a   c. Christian   d. *She doesn't specifically say.*

Matching

MSA	LCA	English
اِبْتدى	ما فيه حدا	(he) doesn't care
أنَّ	هلّا	(he) doesn't give a damn
الآنَ	بسّ	a little (bit); a few
أوْ	كمان	also; too
أيْضًا	كْثير	among us; we have
تجِدُ	عنّا	and then
جِدًّا	شِوَّية	but; only
الّذي، الّتي	هذي	heedless
طائِش	وبعْدَيْن	no one
عِنْدنا	بْتِلاقي	now
قليلًا	بدّهُم يعْملوا	or
لا أحَدَ	اِلْلي	that; who; which
لا يُهِمُّهُ *(x2)*	هدول	that…
لكِن	مِش هامُّه	these (people)
هذِهِ	طاحِش	they want to do
هؤُلاء	مِش عنْدُه فرْقانة	this; these
وثُمَّ	ولّا	to begin
يُريدونَ أنْ يفْعلوا	إنّه	very
	بلِّش	you (can) find

Answers

Main Idea: a **True or False:** 1. F[6] 2. T[7] 3. T[11-12] 4. T[26,30] 5. F[35] **Multiple Choice:** 1. a[4-5] 2. c[17-18] 3. c[26-27] 4. d[29-33] 5. d
Matching: ما فيه حدا no one لا أحَدَ / هلّا now الآنَ / بسّ but; only لكِن / كمان also; too أيْضًا / كْثير very جِدًّا / عنّا among us; we have بدّهُم / تجِدُ you (can) find بْتِلاقي / وثُمَّ and then وبعْدَيْن / هذِهِ this; these هذي / قليلًا a little (bit); a few شِوَّية / عِنْدنا have مِش هامُّه these (people) هؤُلاء / هدول these (people) اِلْلي that; who; which يُريدونَ أنْ يفْعلوا / اِلْلي they want to do بِعْملوا (he) doesn't care لا يُهِمُّهُ / ولّا or أوْ / إنّه that… أنَّ

Text

الدّين في الأُرْدُنّ هُوَ مُسْلِم ومَسيحي.	1	Religion in Jordan is Muslim and Christian.
المُسْلِم بِمارس طُقوسُه الدّينية بِكُلّ راحة مِثل الصّلاة والصّيام والحِجاب	2	Muslims practice their religious rituals comfortably, such as praying, fasting, and [wearing] the hijab.
ما فيه حدا بِيفْرُض عَلَيْه أيّ نَوْع مِن الضُّغوطات.	3*	No one puts any kind of pressure on them.
المسيحي نِفْس الشَّيْء.	4	The same goes for Christians.
بِصلّي بالكنيسة وبِصوم وبِيتْعبّد بِدون ااه... أيّ حدا يِزْعجُه.	5*	They pray at church, and fast, and worship without uh... without any pressures.
والمُسْلِم والمسيحي عادةً في الأُرْدُنّ بِتْعايِشوا بِكُلّ محبّة واحْترام.	6	Muslims and Christians usually live in friendship and respect in Jordan.
هلّأ بالنِّسبة للطّوائِف، يعْني مِش كْثير باعْرِف عن الطّوائِف المسيحية،	7	Now, as for sects, there's not much I know about the Christian sects.
بسّ هيّ مِثل الأرْثوذُكْس والرّوم الكاثوليك واللّاتين وهُمَّ مَوجودين في الأُرْدُنّ	8*	But there are, for example, Orthodox, Roman Catholic and Latin, which are present in Jordan
وعايْشين مَعَ بَعض و... وكُلّ واحِد مِنْهُم عنْدُه الكنيسة تبعْتُه.	9	and co-exist with each other and they each have their own churches and (forms of) worship.
كمان ااه... كمان نِفْس الشَّيْء المُسْلِمين. المُسْلِمين فيه مِنْهُم سِنّيين وفيه مِنْهُم شيعة.	10	It's also the same for Muslims. Some are Sunni, some are Shi'a.
مُعْظ... مُعْظم الـ... يعْني مُعْظم المُسْلِمين الـ... ااه... في الأُرْدُنّ هُمَّ سِنّيين	11	Most... you know... most Muslims... most Muslims in Jordan are Sunni,
وكْثير قليل مِن الشّيعة مِتْواجْدين عنّا ااه... في الـ... في الأُرْدُنّ.	12	and there are very few Shi'a among us uh... in Jordan.
وإذا... إذا وِجدوا يعْني إذا... إذا صار إذا كـ... صار وكانوا مَوْجودين فهُم شِوَّية يعْني أقَلّية. ما إلْهُم أيّ سُلْطة على أيّ حدا.	13	And if... if there are any, they are few; that is, a minority and do not have any power over anyone.
ااه... هلّأ بالنِّسبة لِلتّقاليد الدّينية في بْلادْنا، أكْتر شَيْء بِتْبيّن ااه... في شهْر رمضان لأنّه كُلّ النّاس بِتْكون صايْمة	14	Uh... now, as for religious traditions in our country, the most significant one is in the month of Ramadan where everybody is fasting.
وبِهذي الأيّام الصّيام بِقْعُد شَيْء أرْبعْطشر ساعة لأن النّهار طْويل	15	And these days the fasting is for some fourteen hours because the days are long.
وبِتْلاقي النّاس تعْبانين وعطْشانين. ااه... لكِنّهُم مُلْتزمين بالدّين.	16	And you find the people tired and thirsty, uh... but they abide by the religion.
يعْني حتّى إنّه إخْوانّا المسيحية بِيحْترموا هذي التّقاليد تبعْتِنا	17	Even our Christian brothers respect these traditions of ours;
وبِيتْجنّبوا الأكل في الـ... في الطُّرقات والـ... والمحلّات الـ... العامّة.	18	they avoid eating in the streets and public places.

أحْلى تقاليد شعائري عنّا هُوَّ ساعِة الإفْطار في رمضان	19	The most beautiful ritualistic tradition here is at the hour of iftar during Ramadan, which is at the time of the sunset prayer where everybody gathers around one table and the whole family eats together.
لمّا وقْت صلاة المغْرب لمّا الكُلّ بِيجْتِمِع على سُفْرة واحْدة وبِياكُلوا مَعَ بعْض كُلّ العايْلة.	20	
وبعْدها بِيرْتاحوا شوَيّ وبعْدَيْن بِيروحوا على صلاة التّراويح في المساجِد.	21*	And after that, they rest for a while and then go to the Tarawih prayers in the mosques.
وبتْلاقي النّاس بالطُّرقات في أوْقات مِتأخِّرة مِن اللَّيْل والدُّنْيا عجْقة وحِلْوة ومبْسوطين.	22	And you find people in the streets late into the night and it's crowded and nice and joyous.
هلّأ بالنِّسْبة للجيل الجديد، هلّأ الجيل الجديد نوْعَيْن،	23	Now, as for the new generation, now, there are two kinds of new generation:
مِنْهم اِللي مُلْتزِم بالأخْلاق الدّينية و... ولكنُه مُتحضِّر وبِتعامِل مَعَ النّاس بِكُلّ محبّة واِحْترام وتقْدير	24	those who abide by religious ethics but they're civilized and deal with people with the utmost kindness, respect, and appreciation.
وبِتْلاقيهُم مِفكِّرين ومُنْتِجين وبِدّهُم يعْملوا أيّ شيْء للمُسْتقْبل وللمُجْتمع	25	You find them intellectual and productive and wanting to do anything for the future and society.
وبِشوفوا كُلّ التّطوُّرات والتّقدُّم الحضاري اِللي مَوْجود بالغرْب وبأمْريكا،	26	They observe all the developments and progress of civilization in the West and America,
بسّ بِياخْذوا بسّ الأشْياء اِللي بتِمْشي مَعَ عقيدِتْهُم الدّينية، إن كانت مسيحية أو مُسْلمة.	27	but only take what is in line with their religious beliefs, be they Christian or Muslim.
وهدول عم يِكْتروا هالأيّام في الأُردُنّ.	28	These [types] are growing in number these days in Jordan.
النوْع الثّاني نوْع طاحِش، مِش هامُّه الأخْلاق.	29	The second kind is heedless and doesn't care about morals.
بِياخُذ مِن الـ... مِن الغرْب وأمْريكا أسْوء العادات وبِطبّقْها في بُلادْنا بِدون أيّ تفْكير بالنّاس التّانين،	30	They take the worst customs from the West and America and put them into practice in our country without any thought to other people,
ولّا حتّى أهْله ولا بالمُسْتقْبل ولا بِطوّر حاله، بسّ عشان يِكون "كول" حسب ما بِيحْكوا.	31	or even their families, the future, or their own self-development, rather just to be "cool", as they say.
وحتّى لوْ أخذ فِكْرة مُفيدة مِن الـ... مِن أمَيرْيكا بِيعْملْها بِطريقة كِثير مِش... مِش مِتماشْية مَعَ العادات والتّقاليد العربية.	32	And even if they take a good idea from the... America, they do it in such a way that's really not... not in line with Arab customs and traditions,
و... ومِش هامّة، مِش فرْقانة عنْده وبِيشْكي إنُّه العالم العربي مِش فاهِم علَيْه.	33	and... and they don't care, they don't give a damn, and they complain that the Arab world doesn't understand them.
أنا بسّ باحُبّ أضيف إشَيْ،	34	I'd like to add something.
إنُّه بِرأْي إنُّه الدّين بِينْحِصِر وبِبلِّش وبِيوضح بالأخْلاق.	35	In my opinion, religion consists of, starts with, and becomes clear by ethics.
فإذا كانت أخْلاقْنا كُوَيّسة وراقية ومِنهْتم بالآخر	36	If our ethics are good and of a high standard, and we are concerned about others

ومِنْحافِظ على حُرّيثْنا ااه... وحُرّية النّاس بِغَضّ النّظر إنُّه مسيحي أوْ مُسْلِم	37	and preserve our freedom and the freedom of others regardless whether [we are] Muslims or Christians,
ااه... الأخْلاق هِيَّ... هِيَّ بِتِبْني البني آدميين	38	uh... ethics develop human beings.
ووقْتْها مُمارْسة الطُّقوس مِثْل الصّلاة والصّيام والحجّ والزّكاة ااه... بِتْساعِد النّاس إنُّه يْكمِّل أخْلاقْهُم	39	And then the practice of rituals such as prayer, fasting, pilgrimage, and alms-giving help people to perfect their ethics.
وفيه مقولة عنّا بالدّين الاسْلامي بِتْقول "أنَّ الصّلاةَ تنْهى عن الفحْشاء والمُنْكر."	40	We have this saying in Islam, "Prayer forbids indecency and dishonor."
شُكّرًا.	41	Thank you.

Notes

*3 Levantine Arabic, as many other dialects of Arabic, adds the prefix بـ *b-* to mark the present tense.

*5 The 3rd person masculine prefix يـ is usually dropped when the present tense prefix بِـ is added.

*8 Roman Catholic and Latin are actually one and the same sect.

*21 The Tarawih prayers are non-compulsory prayers in the evenings during Ramadan.

ⓘ Wikipedia *Religion in Jordan:* **bit.ly/1wvrFcA**

University Life

Key Words

اِلْتحقَ، يلْتحِقُ بـ to enter; get into	فصْل دِراسي semester
سكَن housing; residence	كُلّية school; college

Main Idea

   a. Islam explains how the university system works in Egypt.
   b. Islam recounts some funny college experiences.
   c. Islam describes some difficulties about university life.
   d. Islam compares university life in Egypt to that of the West.

True or False

   1. Islam recently graduated from university.
   2. Islam's older siblings had told him how difficult university life was.
   3. There were 450 students in Islam's freshman class.
   4. Islam's daily commute from home to school was ninety minutes.
   5. Islam still lives in off-campus housing.

Multiple Choice

1. Islam is studying ___.

     a. medicine   c. engineering
     b. nursing   d. *none of the above*

2. Islam's mom and dad were ___ when he got into his faculty.

     a. happy   c. worried
     b. disappointed   d. surprised

3. Students are accepted into the dormitories based on ___ and ___.

     a. their family's income   c. how far their families live from campus
     b. their grades   d. the faculty they've been accepted into

4. Islam moved into campus dorms at the ___ semester of his freshman year.

     a. beginning of his first   c. beginning of his second
     b. end of his first   d. end of his second

5. What does Islam find difficult about college?

     a. attending lectures   c. living in the dorms
     b. the time required to study   d. university life in general

Matching

الغالِبِية العُظْمى مِن	and so forth; etc.
وهكذا دوالَيْك	day by day
على الإطْلاق	finally
أخيرًا	however
بِمُرور الأيّام	I don't need
غَيْرَ أنّ	later; at a later time
أبَدًا	never
حَيْثُ	(not) at all
ومِن سوءِ حظّي	so
فـ	the vast majority of
لا أحْتاجُ إلى	unfortunately
في وقْتٍ لاحِق	where

Answers

Main Idea: c **True or False:** 1. F[2] 2. T[4-6] 3. T[14] 4. T[21] 5. F[35-37] **Multiple Choice:** 1. c[10] 2. a[11] 3. b[27] & c 4. c[35] 5. d[39]

Matching: الغالِبِية العُظْمى مِن the vast majority of / وهكذا دوالَيْك and so forth; etc. / على الإطْلاق (not) at all / أخيرًا finally / بِمُرور الأيّام day by day / غَيْرَ أنّ however / أبَدًا never / حَيْثُ where / ومِن سوءِ حظّي unfortunately / فـ so / لا أحْتاجُ إلى I don't need / في وقْتٍ لاحِق later; at a later time

Text

مرْحبًا بِكُم.	1	Hi, everyone.
أحِبُّ أنْ أذكِرُكُم بِأنّي طالِبٌ جامِعي في السّنةِ الثّانية لي في الجامِعة.	2	I want to remind you that I am a college student in my second year of college.
ااااه... أوَدُّ أوّلًا أنْ أخْبِرَكُم كَيْفَ كُنْتُ أتخيّلُ الحَياة الجامِعية قبْلَ الإلتحاقِ بها.	3	Uh... I'd first like to tell how I had imagined university life before I entered it.
ااااه... لَدَيَّ أخٌ في كُلِّية الطّب وأُخْتٌ في كُلِّية التّمْريض	4	Uh... I have a brother in medical school and a sister in nursing school,
فكانَ كُلُّ ما أعْلمُهُ أو الغالِبِية العُظْمى مِنْهُ عن الجامِعة يأْتي مِنْهُما.	5	so everything I knew--or the vast majority of it--about university came from them.
"فالحَياة الجامِعة صعْبة لِلغاية والدِّراسة لَيْست سهْلة وتحْتاجُ لِلمُذاكرةِ طيلة الوقْت" وهكذا دوالَيْك.	6	"University life is really tough and the classes are not easy, and you have to study all the time," and so forth.
هكذا كانا يقولانِ لي	7	This is what they used to always tell me,

دائمًا حتّى اعتقدتُ في نفسي أنّني مُقبِل على عالمٍ مِنَ الصُّعوبات الّتي لن أستطيعَ تحمُّلَها.	8	to the point that I thought to myself that I was going to a world full of challenges that I wouldn't be able to handle.
وانتظرتُ ذلكَ اليَوم.	9	I waited for that day.
ااه... ذلكَ اليَوم الّذي علمتُ فيه بأنّني التحقتُ بكُلّية الهندسة كانَ يَومًا رائعًا.	10	Uh... The day I found out that I had gotten into the faculty of engineering was a great day.
سعِدَ أبي وأمّي وأنا أيضًا كُنتُ سعيدًا بهذا الخبَر.	11	My dad and mom were happy, and I was happy too, to hear that news.
التحقتُ بإحدى الجامعات تُدعى جامعة كفر الشَّيخ ااه... في ااه...	12	I had gotten into one of colleges called Kafr El-Sheikh... in....
لم يكُن أوّل يَومٌ مُميّزًا على الإطلاق.	13	The first day wasn't special at all.
فقد كانَ عدد رُبْعُمية وخمسين... رُبْعُمية وخمسين... وخمسون طالبًا يسألونَ نفْس السُّؤال:	14*	There were four hundred and fifty students asking the same question.
ماذا نفْعل؟ ماذا نفْعل؟	15	"What should we do? What should we do?"
وبالطَّبع كُنتُ أحدُهُم.	16	And of course I was one of them.
كما أنّهُم جميعًا كانَ يظْهرُ عليْهِم نفْسُ الشُّعور، شُعور الفرْحةِ العارمة	17	They also all had the same feelings, feelings of euphoria,
كما لَو أنّهُم يقولون "أخيرًا أصْبحْتُ طالبًا جامعيًّا."	18	as if they were saying, "Finally, I've become a university student."
بـ... بمُرور الأيّام علمنا طريقة سيْر العمل في الكُلّية،	19	Day by day we learned the ins-and-outs of college.
غَيْرَ أنّنا ااه... بدأْنا... أو بدأْتُ أنا أشْعرُ بالتَّعب حَيثُ أنّني أتحرّكُ من بيْتي	20	However, we began... or I began, to feel tired, as I was traveling from home
ااه... إلى الكُلّية ما يقْرُبُ من ساعة ونصْف... يسْتهْلِكُني الطَّريقُ ساعةً ونصْف.	21	uh... to school, which was an hour and a half away... The trip would take me an hour and a half.
ثُمّ أقْضي مُحاضراتي والّتي في بعْضِ الأيّام قد ااه... تنتهي في السّادسة مساءً.	22	Then I attended my lectures, which on some days might, uh... finish at six in the evening.
ثُمّ ااه... أسْتغْرِقُ ساعةً ونصْفَ أخرى حتّى أعودَ إلى البَيت.	23	Then I'd spend another hour and half to get back home.
فلم أكُن أجِدُ الوقْتَ الكافي أبدًا للمُذاكرة وكذلكَ لا يُفارقُني الإرْهاق.	24	I never found enough time to study and I always felt tired.
وكانَ كُلّ ذلكَ بسبب ااه... السّكن الطُّلابي، أو كما نُسمّيه المدينة الجامعية.	25	All of this was because of the dormitories, or as we call them, "the university town".
فقد كانوا ااه... كان الطُّلاب يذْهبونَ إلى تلكَ المدينة الجامعية ااه... حَيثُ يُقْبلونَ مِن مبدأيْن اثْنَيْن ألا وهُما:	26	They would... the students would go to that university town, where they would be accepted based on two criteria, namely:
النِّسْبة المئَوية أوْ التَّقْدير وثانيهُما، ااه... بُعْد المسافة عنِ الكُلّية.	27	their grades or evaluation, and secondly how far he is from the college.

ومِن سوءِ حظّي أنّني لم أحْصُل على أيٍّ مِنْهُما،	28	Unfortunately, I didn't meet either of the two,
فلم ألْتحِقْ بِالمدينةِ الجامعية في الفصلِ الدِّراسي الأوّلِ،	29	so I didn't get into the dorms during my first semester,
فاضْطررْتُ في البِدايةِ... في أوّلِ فصلٍ دراسي أنْ أشْترِكَ معَ بعْضِ أصْدِقائي في تأجيرِ سكنٍ خارِجي، بِالقُرْبِ مِنَ الجامعة	30	so in the beginning... in my first semester, I had to rent a place with some of my friends near the university,
وما أدْراكَ ما السّكن الخارِجي.	31	what everyone knows as "off-campus" housing.
ااه... أحِبُّ أنْ أسمّي الطّالبَ الّذي يسْكُنُ خارِجَ المدينةِ بِالطّالبِ المِسْكين،	32	I like to refer to students who live off campus as "the pitiable students"
فهُوَ الّذي يطْبُخُ ويكْنِسُ ويُنظِّفُ ويُرتِّبُ ويشْتري الطّعامَ ويدْفعُ الإيجارَ ويُشاركُ رُفقاءهُ في السّكنِ في كُلِّ شَيْء.	33	because they are the ones who cook, sweep, clean, tidy up, buy food, pay for rent, and do everything with their roommates.
لقد كانَ فصلًا دِراسيًّا عصيبًا،	34	It was a very difficult semester.
ثُمّ تقدّمْتُ بِالتِماسٍ في بِدايةِ الفصْلِ الدِّراسي الثّاني	35	Then I applied to the dorms again at the beginning of the second semester
وحمْدًا لله تمّ قُبولي به.	36	and, praise God, I was accepted.
فوجدْتُ طعامي جاهِزًا بِمَوْعِدِهِ وغُرْفتي جاهِزة	37	I found my food ready at its time and my room was ready;
ولا أحْتاجُ إلى أيِّ شَيْءٍ غَيْرَ أغْراضي الشّخْصية.	38	I didn't need anything but my personal stuff.
ااه... مِن تِلْكَ السّنةِ الّتي قضَيْتُها... مِنَ السّنةِ والنِّصْف... علمْتُ بِأنّ الدِّراسةَ الجامعية لَيست هِيَ وجْهُ الصُّعوبةِ ولكِنّها الحَياةُ الجامعية نفْسُها.	39	From the year... year and a half... I've spent [at college], I've learned that the university courses are not the difficult part, but [rather] university life itself.
تلْكَ لَيست القِصّة الكامِلة لكِن أتمنّى أنْ تكون قد أثارتِ انْتِباهَكُم.	40	This is not the entire story, but I hope it attracted your attention.
أراكُم في وقْتٍ لاحِق.	41	See you later.

Notes

*14 Native speakers often have difficulties deciding when they should use ـون instead of ـين with numbers (20, 30, etc.), as their native dialects use only ـين.

The Arabic Language

Key Words

الفُصْحى Standard Arabic   لِهْجة dialect

Main Idea

a. Lilia explains how regional dialects evolved from Standard Arabic.
b. Lilia describes the situation in the Arab world with Standard Arabic and regional dialects.
c. Lilia argues why regional dialects should replace Standard Arabic as official languages.
d. Lilia focuses on some peculiarities among the regional dialects of Tunisia.

True or False

1. Arabic has a rich structure and complex morphology.
2. Lilia mentions that several consonants in Tunisian Arabic are pronounced differently than those in Standard Arabic.
3. In Tunisia, newspapers are published in both French and the Tunisian dialect.
4. Lilia gives examples of the phrase "What do you want?" in various dialects.
5. Lilia believes that Standard Arabic should remain the official language.

Multiple Choice

1. Lilia believes that the existence of local dialects ___.

    a. makes learning Arabic difficult for foreigners
    b. is unfortunate
    c. is a result of European colonialism
    d. makes the Arabic language rich and interesting

2. The Tunisian dialect is ___.

    a. difficult for Egyptians to understand, whereas Tunisians can easily understand Egyptians.
    b. difficult for Egyptians to understand, and vice versa.
    c. easy for Egyptians to understand, whereas Tunisians have difficulty understanding Egyptians.
    d. difficult for Egyptians to understand, but easy for Lebanese.

3. Lilia mentions a nickname for Standard Arabic: ___.

    a. The Language of the Media   c. The Language of Al-Daad
    b. The Language of God   d. The Semitic Language

4. Standard Arabic differs from most other languages in the world because ___.

    a. it is not used in oral communication   c. it is the official language of
    b. it is threatened with extinction   dozens of countries
                                                  d. *all of the above*

5. Lilia thinks that Standard Arabic ___.

    a. contains too many obscene words these days
    b. should be replace English as the international language
    c. will one day replace local dialects and unite all Arabs
    d. is in danger of extinction

Matching

تعْتبرُ	and that's because…
مِنَ الناحِية	completely
معَ الأسفِ الشّديد	etc.; and so on
إلى آخِرِهِ	for example
في حَينٍ	hasn't… yet
تمَامًا	in addition to this, …
على سبيلِ المِثال	in terms of
مِنَ الصعْبِ على	it is considered
فإنَّ هذا لا ينْفي أنَّ	it's hard for…
وذلِكَ لِأنَّ	just as
بِفضْل	must
على عكْسِ	thanks to
لمْ… بعْدُ	that's not to deny that…
عِلاوةً عن هذا فإنَّ	unfortunately
لا بُدَّ أنْ	unlike
تمَامًا كـ	whereas; while

Answers

Main Idea: b **True or False:** 1. T[2] 2. F[16] 3. F[14-15] 4. T[21] 5. T **Multiple Choice:** 1. b[6] 2. a[18] 3. c[27] 4. a[30] 5. d[37]
Matching: تعْتبرُ it is considered / مِنَ الناحِية in terms of / معَ الأسفِ الشّديد unfortunately / إلى آخِرِهِ etc.; and so on / في حَينٍ whereas; while / تمَامًا completely / على سبيلِ المِثال for example / مِنَ الصعْبِ على it's hard for… / فإنَّ هذا لا ينْفي أنَّ that's not to deny that… / وذلِكَ لِأنَّ and that's because… / بِفضْل thanks to / على عكْسِ unlike / لمْ… بعْدُ hasn't… yet / عِلاوةً عن هذا فإنَّ in addition to this, … / لا بُدَّ أنْ must / تمَامًا كـ just as

Text

تعْتبرُ اللّغةِ العربية مِن أهمِّ لُغاتِ العالمِ	1	Arabic is considered one of the most important languages of the world,
وأغْناها تركِّيبًا وأكْثرِها تعْقِيدًا، اااه... خاصّةً مِنَ الناحِية المورْفولوجية (أوْ عِلْم التّشكُّل).	2	the richest of them in structure, and the most complex, uh... especially in terms of morphology (or the science of word formation).
وكيْفَ لا؟	3	And how could it not [be]?
وهِيَ لُغة الإعْجاز ولُغة القُرآنِ الكريم.	4	It is the language of miracles and the language of the Holy Quran.
وهِيَ اللُّغةُ الرّسْمية لِكُلِّ دُوَلِ العالمِ العربي.	5	It is the official language of all the countries of the Arab world.
ولكِن معَ الأسف الشّديد، فإنَّ لِكُلِّ بلدٍ عربيٍّ لهْجةً محلّية، مُميِّزة لَهُ.	6	But unfortunately, every Arab country has its local dialect, distinct to it.
حيْثُ نجِدُ اللهْجةَ المصْرية، السّورية، الجزائِرية، اممم... الكُويْتية، إلى آخِره.	7	And so, we find the Egyptian, Syrian, Algerian, and Kuwaiti dialects, and so on.
بعْضَ اللّهجات تكونُ سهْلةُ الفهْم بِالنّسْبة لِمُعْظمِ العرب، كالمِصْرية مثلًا.	8	Some dialects are easy to understand for most Arabs, like Egyptian, for example,
في حَيْن تعْتبرُ اللّهجات المغارِبية أكْثرَ تعْقيدًا، اممم... وأعْسرَ فهْمًا، كالتّونِسية والجزائِرية.	9	while the Maghreb dialects are considered more puzzling, and mmm... difficult to understand, like Tunisian and Algerian.
فاللّهجات المغارِبية تخْتلِفُ تمامًا عن اللّهجات العربية الشّرْق أوْسطية.	10	The Maghreb dialects are quite different from the Arabic dialects of the Middle East.
اااه... تكونُ مُخْتلِف اللّهجات العربية مُشْتقّةً مِنَ اللُّغة العربية الفُصْحى...	11	Uh... the various Arabic dialects are derived from classical Arabic...
وممْزوجةً بِعِدّة لُغاتٍ أخْرى دخيلة تعْكِسُ تاريخَ وحضارة البلد المعْني.	12	and mixed with several other foreign languages that reflect the history and culture of the country concerned.
وعلى سبيلِ المِثال، فاللّهْجة التّونِسية (أوْ الدّارِجة) مُتكوِّنة بِالإضافة إلى العربية الفُصْحى، مِنَ الفرنسية، والتُّركية، والإيطالية والأمازيغية (أوالبرْبرية).	13	So for example, the Tunisian dialect (or "the vernacular") consists of—in addition to classical Arabic—French, Turkish, Italian and Tamazight (or Berber).
وتُسْتعْملُ الدّارِجة في أغْلبِ الإذاعاتِ والقنَوات، ولكِن ليْسَ في الصُّحُف،	14	The vernacular is used on most radio stations and [TV] channels, but not in newspapers.
فهذِه الأخيرة تكونُ إمّا بِالعربية الفُصْحى أوْ بِالفرنسية.	15	This last one [i.e. newspapers] is either in classical Arabic or French.
والمُميِّز في اللّهْجة التّونِسية اااه... هُوَ النُّطْقُ الصّحيح لِكُلِّ الحُروف العربية الثّمانية والعشرين	16*	The defining feature of the Tunisian dialect uh... is the correct pronunciation of the Arabic letters for each twenty-eight characters,
بِما فيهِم حرْف الجيم، والذّال، والضّاد، والقاف... الّتي لا تُنْطق في اللّهجات الأُخْرى.	17	including ج and ذ and ض and ق... which are not pronounced [correctly] in other dialects.

كما إنّهُ مِنَ السّهْلِ على التّونسي فهْم المِصْري أوِ اللُّبْناني، في حينٍ، يجِدُ المِصْري واللُّبْناني صُعوبةً في فهْمِ اللّهْجة التّونسية.	18	It is easy for Tunisians to understand Egyptians or the Lebanese, while Egyptians and the Lebanese find it difficult to understand the Tunisian dialect.
كما مِنَ الصّعْبِ على التّونسي فهْمِ اللّهجاتِ الخليجية،	19	Likewise, it is difficult for Tunisians to understand the Gulf dialects,
وهُوَ ما يسْتدْعي الإسْتِعانةَ باللُّغة العربية الفُصْحى لِتسْهيلِ عمليةِ التّواصِلِ والفهْمِ بيْنَ العرب.	20	which calls for help from classical Arabic to facilitate communication and understanding between Arabs.
فمثلًا جُمْلة "ماذا تُريد؟" تُتْرجَمُ كالتّالي في مُخْتلِفِ اللّهجات.	21	For example, the phrase "What do you want?" is translated as follows in different dialects.
بالمِصْري: "إنت عايز أيْه؟"،	22	In Egyptian: "inta 3āyiz ʔēh?";
باللّيبي: "شْتِبي؟"،	23	in Libyan: "štibi?";
باللُّبْناني: "شو بدّك؟"،	24	in Lebanese: "šū baddak?";
وبالتّونسي: "شِتْحِبّ؟"... حَيْثُ يكونُ الإخْتِلافُ واضِحًا.	25	and in Tunisian: "š-ithibb?"... whereby the difference is clear.
ورغْمَ أن هذا الإخْتِلاف في اللّهجاتِ العربية يعْكِسُ اااه... ويُجذِّرُ تاريخَ وحضارةَ كُلِّ بلدٍ،	26	Although this difference in Arabic dialects reflects uh... and goes to the roots of the history and culture of each country,
فإنَّ هذا لا ينْفي أنَّ "لُغة الضّاد" مُهدَّدة بالإنْدِثار!	27*	this is not to deny that the "Language of *Al-Daad*" is threatened with extinction!
وذلِكَ لِأنّها غَيْرَ محْكية،	28	And that's because it isn't spoken.
فجميعُ لُغاتُ العالمِ تصْمُدُ بفضْلِ عمليةِ التّكلُّم،	29	All the languages of the world endure, thanks to the speech process [i.e. the fact that they're spoken],
على عكْسِ اللُّغةِ العربية الّتي أُسْتُغْنِيَ عنْها في التّواصلِ الشّفَوي.	30	unlike [classical] Arabic, which is done away with in oral communication.
فمِنَ الغريبِ أنْ لا يتكلّمَ العربُ لُغتَهُم الفُصْحى!	31	It is strange that the Arabs do not speak their standard language!
ومِنَ الأغْربِ أنّهُم لا يتعرّضونَ لها سِوى في المدارِس، والكُتُب و... الصُّحف و... أحْيانًا في التِّلفاز عِنْدَ نشْراتِ الأنْباء.	32	And what's stranger is that they are only exposed to it in schools, books and... newspapers, and... sometimes on television during news broadcasts.
وفي نفْسِ الوقْت، الكثيرونَ يُفضِّلونَ جعْلَ اللّهْجة المحلّية لُغةً رسْمية.	33	At the same time, there are many people who would prefer to make the local dialect the official language.
ففي تونس مثلًا اممم... ظهرتِ العديد مِنَ الكِتابات بالدّارجة.	34	In Tunisia, for example, uh... many writings have appeared in the 'vernacular'
وحتّى أنّها تحْتَوي على عِباراتٍ "بذيئة" ورُبّما تخْدُشُ بالحَياء!	35	and they even contain 'obscene' words and maybe indecent acts!
لِذلِكَ فأنا شخْصيًا ضِدَّ جعْلَ اللّهْجة العامية رسْمية،	36	Therefore, I am personally against making the dialect official,
خاصّةً وأنَّ اللُّغة العربية الفُصْحى مُهدَّدة بالإنْقِراض،	37	especially since classical Arabic is threatened with extinction,

ونحْنُ العربُ لم نتمكّن بعْدُ مِن إتْقانِها كُلِّيًا،	38	and we Arabs have not yet been able to master it entirely,
فمِنَ الصّعْبِ الإلْمامِ بِجميع قَواعِدِها والإحاطةِ بِمبادِئِها.	39	as it is difficult to be knowledgeable in all its rules of grammar and to be familiar with its principles .
و... عِلاوةً عن هذا فإنّ اللُّغةَ الرسْمية لا بُدَّ أنْ تكونَ لُغةً ساميةً، نقيةً وراقِية، تمامًا كاللُّغةَ العربية الفُصْحى.	40	And... In addition to this, the official language must be a Semitic language, pure and elegant, just as the language of classical Arabic.

Notes

*16 This is mostly true. However, a distinct feature of Tunisian Arabic is that ض is pronounced as ظ [ðˤ].

*27 لُغةَ الضّاد (Language of Al-Daad) is a nickname among Arabs for their language, as the sound of the letter ض is seen as being particularly unique to the Arabic language.

ⓘ Wikipedia *Diglossia:* **bit.ly/1xfEaak**

Technology

Key Words

التِّكْنولوجيا technology | التَّواصِل الاِجْتِماعي social networking
تلفون ذكي smart phone | مُتطَوِّر evolving

Main Idea

Razanne talks about ___.

- a. the astonishing rate at which smart phones and social networks have evolved in recent years
- b. both positive and negative aspects of smart phones and social networks
- c. only positive aspects of smart phones and social networks
- d. only negative aspects of smart phones and social networks

True or False

1. Razanne has an iPhone.
2. Razanne mentions that it's annoying how people play on their phones and ignore people they're sitting at a table with.
3. Razanne implies that many people overshare on social networking sites.
4. Because of Facebook, people can better remember other people's birthdays.
5. Commenting on photos and updates is a good way to keep in touch with friends.

Multiple Choice

1. Razanne feels her smart phone ___ and ___.

   - a. connects her to the world
   - b. makes her laptop useless
   - c. makes her more anti-social
   - d. makes her memory weaker

2. Razanne mainly uses ___ to keep up with her friends and relatives in Syria.

   - a. Facebook   b. Google+   c. Skype   d. telephone calls

3. Razanne has one friend in particular who ___.

   - a. posts pictures of practically every meal she eats
   - b. posts things like "I need to use the bathroom!"
   - c. "likes" everything on Razanne's Facebook newsfeed, but never comments
   - d. never goes out anymore, but rather stays home and plays on Facebook

4. Since we never need to dial numbers these days, Razanne can only remember ___.

   - a. 911
   - b. her own number
   - c. her husband's number
   - d. her parents' number

5. Razanne wishes people would ___ and ___.

    a.   use simple messaging apps like WhatsApp instead of Facebook

    b.   call each other on the phone more

    c.   correspond through hand-written letters like in the past

    d.   meet up in person instead of messaging from home

Matching

MSA	LCA	English
أُريدُ	هلّأ	anyone
الآنَ	لح نِحْكي	but
أيّ شخْصٍ	فيه إلْها	don't; doesn't
جميل	بِدّي	for; to
سَأتكَّمُ	نِحْنا	he has
لِ	أيّ حدا	I want
لا	ما	I'll speak
لا يزالُ	بيِقْدر	it lets me
لكِن	مْنيح	like that; that way
لها	هَيْك	nice, good
لَيْسَ	لِ	not
المرْء	هُنَيْك	now
نحْنُ	لهلّأ	one; you
هكذا	بِخلّيني	she has; it has
هُناكَ	بسّ	still
يسْتطيعُ	الواحِد	there
يُمكّنُني	مو	we
دخلَ، يدْخُلُ	عال	because
على الـ	فات، يفوت	how much?
كانَ مِنَ المُمْكِنِ أنْ نرى	لَيْش؟	if only...
كم؟	أدَيْش؟	on the __
لأنَّ	باعْتِبار إنّه	to enter
لماذا؟	كنّا مُمْكِن نشوف	to put
لَيْتَ	حطّ، يحُطّ	we could see
وضعَ، يضعُ	يا رَيْت لَوْ	why?

Answers

Main Idea: b **True or False:** 1. T[27] 2. F 3. T[23-26] 4. F[34-35] 5. F[41-43] **Multiple Choice:** 1. a[7] & d[30] 2. a[14-15] 3. b[23] 4. b[31]
5. b[42] & d **Matching:** هلّأ now / الآنَ now / لح نِحْكي I'll speak / سَأتكُمْ / فيه إلها she has; it has / لها / بِدّي I want / أُريدُ / نِحْنا we / نَحْنُ / أيّ
لـ / هَيْك like that; that way / هكذا / أيّ شخْصٍ ما / لا don't; doesn't / بِيُقدر / he has بِيمُلُك / يَستطيعُ / مْنيح nice, good / جميل / هَيْك like that; that way / هكذا / لـ / anyone حدا
for; to / لـ / هُنِّيك there / هُناك / لهلّأ still لا يزالُ / بِخلّيني it lets me / يُمَكِّنُني / بَسّ but لكِن / المْرء / الواحد one; you / لَيْسَ not مو / عالـ on
the / على الـ ___ / يفوت، فات to enter فاتَ / دخلَ، يدْخُلُ / دخلَ / why? لَيْش؟ / لماذا؟ / أدَيْش؟ how much? كم؟ / باعْتِبار إنّه because / لأنَّ / كُنّا مُمْكِن
نِشوف we could see / نرى أنْ مِنَ المُمْكِنِ / كانَ / حَطّ، بِحُطّ / وضعَ، يضعُ / حَطّ to put / لَوْ if only... لَيْتَ / يا رَيْت لَوْ

Text

هلّأ لح نِحْكي عن التِّكْنولوجيا.	1	Now we're going talk about technology.
التِّكْنولوجيا طبْعًا هِيَّ سِلاح ذو حدَّيْن.	2	Technology is a double-edged sword.
فيه إلْها أُمور إيجابية وفيه إلها أُمور سلْبية.	3	It has both positive and negative aspects.
لمّا بِدّي فكِّر بِعصْر التِّكْنولوجيا اِللي نِحْنا هلّأ عايْشينُه أوّل شَيْء بِخْطر على بالي هُوَّ التّلفونات، التلفونات الذّكية.	4*	When I think about the era of technology we live in, the first thing that comes to my mind is phones, smart phones.
طبْعًا أيّ حدا بِيمُلُك تلفون ذكي ما بِظنّ إنّه بِيقدر يِقْعد بْلاه أكْثر مِن ساعتَيْن.	5	Of course, anyone who owns a smart phone doesn't think he can live without it more than two hours.
هَيّ أنا مِن تجْربة شخْصية، أنا ما باقْدر أقْعد بِدون تلفوني ولا دقيقة حتّى.	6*	From my personal experience, I can't live without my phone even for a minute.
باحِسّ إنّه هُوَّ اِللي بِوصِّلْني للعالم الخارِجي كلُّه.	7	I even feel that it is what connects me to with the world at large.
أيّ شَيْء بِدّي ياه باقْدر أعْملُه على التّلفون.	8	Anything I need to do, I can do with my phone.
امممم... طبْعًا فيه كْثير ناس بِيسْتخْدمُه هَيّ الطّريقة ولكِن... إلها أثر سِلْبي بِصراحة على حَياتْهُن.	9	Um, of course, a lot of people use it this way, but... it has negative effects, frankly, on their lives.
يَعْني لمّا يِكون الواحد عنْدُه الخَيار إنّه يخْرُج مع أصْدِقائُه ويِقْضي وقت مْنيح معهُن ويِطّمنّ عليْهُن فلازِم الواحد يِعْمل هَيْك،	10	For example, when someone has the option to go out with his friends and spend a nice time with them and catch up with them, that's what they should do,
أمّا لمّا يِكون الواحد عنْدُه هدا الخَيار وبِيكْتِفي بَسّ بالتّواصِل معهُن مِن الهاتِف أوْ مِن مَواقِع التّواصِل الاِجْتِماعي فهدا غلط.	11	but when someone has this option and they settle for just communicating with them on the phone or through social networking sites, that's so wrong.
بالنِّسْبة لحالْتي أنا شخْصيًا، أنا عنْدي أهْل كْثير، عائِلة كْبيرة وأصْدِقاء بْسوريا،	12	In my own case, personally, I have lots of people, a large family and friends in Syria,
وبِسبب الأوْضاع الحالية بْسوريا والـ... والحرب اِللي... ااهـ... عم تِصير هُنيك، الكِلّ بِيعْرِفْها،	13	and because of the current situation in Syria and the... the war uh... that's happening over there, as everyone knows, ...
بِسبب هَيّ الأوْضاع أنا باحِبّ إنّي أطّمنّ على رفقاتي وأهْلي اِللي ساكْنين بْسوريا لهلّأ.	14	because of this situation, I like to check on my friends and family who still live in Syria.

طَبْعًا أَكْثَر شَيْء بِخَلِّيني أَطْمَنّ عَلَيْهُن هُوَّ مَواقِع التَّواصُل الاِجْتِماعي أَوْ خَلِّينا نِكون مُحَدِّدين أَكْثَر، مَوْقِع الفَيْس بوك.	15	Of course, the thing that lets me check on them best is social networking websites, or to be more specific, Facebook.
هُوَّ طَريقة مِثالية للواحِد يِقْدر يِتْواصِل ويِطْمَنّ على أَهْلُه بِبلد تانْية.	16	It's the perfect way for someone to be able to stay connected and check on their relatives in another country.
اممم... بِصَراحة هاد بِالنِّسْبة إلي بِحدّ ذاتُه نِعْمة، نِعْمة كِبيرة.	17	Um... to be honest, for me it's a blessing in itself to have this option, a great blessing.
بَسّ بِنَفْس الوَقْت هُوَّ بِالنِّسْبة إلي بِأُمور تانْية نِقْمة.	18	But at the same time it, for me, is an affliction when it comes to other things.
وهَيّ النِّقْمة بِتْكون ااه... النِّقْمة يَعْني الآثار السِّلْبية.	19	And this affliction is... by affliction I mean the negative effects....
هَيّ الآثار السِّلْبية هِيّ إِنُّه الواحِد ما يِكون عِنْدُه خُصوصية كِبيرة،	20	These negative effects are that you don't have a lot of privacy.
الواحِد بِصير لا شُعوريًا بِحُطّ صُوَرُه وبِـ بِشارِك أَخْبارُه مَعَ النّاس.	21	You unintentionally start posting your pictures and sharing news with people.
أنا مو ضِدّ هدا الشَّيْء بَسّ مو دائْمًا.	22	I'm not against this, but not all the time.
بِصَراحة أنا عِنْدي كْثير أَصْدِقاء عالفَيْس بوك يَعْني مُمْكِن إذا بِدْهُن يِروحوا يِفوتوا عالحمّام، بِكْتِبوا إِنُّه أنا فاِيت عالحمّام.	23	To be honest, I have a lot of friends on Facebook who, for example, if they need to go to the bathroom, will post "Gotta use the restroom!"
أَحْيانًا إِنُّه بافكِّر فيها إِنُّه طَيِّب لَيْش عم تِخْبِرْنا؟!	24	Sometimes I think, "Okay, why are you telling us [that]?!"
إِنُّه ااه... فيه كْثير شَغْلات بِسْتَخْدِموها النّاس بِطَريقة زيادة عن اللُّزوم.	25	There are a lot of things people use more than they need to.
يَعْني زيادة اِسْتِخْدام الشَّيْء هُوَّ بِنَظَري أنا حَيْكون سَيِّء قَدّ ما كان هدا الشَّيْء مْنيح.	26	That is, overusing something, in my opinion, can be bad, no matter how good it is.
غَيْر عن هَيْك كمان مَوْضوع... الـ... الـ... التَّلفونات الذَّكية بِذكِّرْني بِمَوْضوع أَدَيْش أنا هدا التِّلفون الذَّكي تبعي (أنا عِنْدي iPhone) أَدَيْش هُوَّ مِريِّحْني بِأُمور مِثْل جَدْوَل المَواعيد،	27	Besides that, another thing about smartphones, which reminds me how much my smart phone--I have an iPhone--how much easier it makes things,
مِثْل ااه... رِفْقاتي... أَعْياد ميلاد رِفْقاتي وعائِلْتي ااه... مِثْل الإيمَيْلات ااه... اِمـ... عناوين الإيمَيْلات تبع الأَصْدِقاء أَوْ الشـ...أَوْ العمل أَوْ أَيّ شَيّ.	28	like appointments, like uh... friends... my friends' and family's birthdays, uh... like e-mails uh... my friends' e-mail addresses, or w... or work or whatever.
كِلّها مَحْفوظة ضِمْن هدا الجِهاز حتى الصُوَر ااه... صُوَري الشَّخْصية اممم... مَوْجودة ضِمْن هدا التِّلفون.	29	Everything is stored in this device, even pictures, personal pictures are found on this phone.
هدا الشَّيْء بِخَلِّي ذاكِرْتي وعَقْلي خاصّةً ذاكِرْتي أنا الشَّخْصية... بِخَلِّيها ااه... ضعيفة.	30	This makes my memory, my mind, especially my memory... it makes it weak.

يَعْني أنا هلّا مُستَحيل أَقْدر أتْذَكّر أيّ رقْم تلفون لأيّ شخص إلّا رقم تلفوني الشّخْصي باعْتِبار إنّه باعْطيه للنّاس.	31	I can't remember anybody's phone number, except my own phone number because I give it to people.
هدا هُوَّ الشّـ... هدا هُوَّ الرّقم الوحيد اِللي أنا باتْذكّرُه.	32	It's the only th... the only number I remember.
وباظُنّ إنّه كِثير مِثْلي عنْدهُن نفْس الوضع.	33	And I think a lot of people are in the same situation.
بَيْنما مِن قَبل كِنّا مُمْكِن نِشوف مِن عشر سْنين أوْ خمْسطْعشر سنة	34	While in the past we could see, ten or fifteen years ago,
كِنّا مُمْكِن نِشوف كِثير مِن النّاس بِقْدروا يِتْذكّروا أرْقام تلفونات بعْضهُن أوْ يِتْذكّروا أعْياد ميلاد بعْضهُن.	35	we could see people who could remember each other's phone numbers or birthdates.
اممم... قصْدي مِن كِلّ هدا الكلام إنّه التّلفونات هَيّ التّكْنولوجيا المُتطوّرة هَيّ وقرّتْلنا أمور ما كِنّا مْنِحْلم فيها مِن قَبل،	36	What I mean is that smartphones and this evolving technology have offered us things we couldn't even dream of in the past,
بسّ كمان بِنفْس الوقت أثّرت على جِسمْنا وأثّرت على ذاكِرتنا للأسف.	37	but at the same time that unfortunately affects our bodies and memories.
أنا باتْمنّى إنّه أرْجع حسّن ذاكِرْتي مِن أوّل وجديد وأرْجع أحْفظ الأرْقام	38	I wish I could start improving my memory again and start memorizing numbers
أوْ المَعْلومات المُهِمّة أوْ مَواعيدي اِللي أنا لازِم أتْقيّد فيها،	39	or important information or my schedules I need to adhere to,
أحْفظها بِذاكِرْتي بدل ما أحْفظها بِذاكِرة التّلفون.	40	and storing information in my memory instead of storing things in my phone's memory.
اممم... كمان باتْمنّى مِن النّاس إنّه ما يْسيّئوا اِسْتِخْدام التّكْنولوجيا أوْ مَواقع التّواصل الاِجْتماعي.	41	Um... Also, I wish that people wouldn't misuse technology and social networks,
ااااه... يِحاوْلوا يِتْواصلوا معَ بعْض أكْثر، يِحاوْلوا يِشوفوا بعْض أكْثر، يِحاوْلوا يِتْصلوا بِبعْض أكْثر	42	uh... that they'd try to communicate with each other and try to see each other more often and call each other more,
وما يِكْتِفوا بسّ بـ... بِرُؤْية الـ... الـ updates عالفَيْس بوك أوْ شو... شو كتبوا وشو حطّوا صُوَر.	43	instead of looking at... updates on Facebook and what... what they write and what pictures they post.
يا رَيْت لَوْ يِقْدروا اممم... يِتْواصلوا معَ بعْض بالحقيقة مِثْل ما بِتْواصلوا معَ بعْض على مَواقع التّواصل الاِجْتماعي أوْ بالـ apps على التّلفونات مِثْل الـ WhatsApp أوْ الـ Viber أوْ ااه... أيّ apps تانْية.	44	If only they could keep in touch with each other in real life the way they keep in touch on social networks or on apps on the phone like WhatsApp or Viber or other apps.
شُكْرًا.	45	Thank you.

Notes

*4 Levantine Arabic, as many other dialects of Arabic, adds the prefix بـ *b-* to mark the present tense. The 3rd person masculine prefix يـ is usually dropped when the present tense prefix بِـ is added.

*6 The negative is formed by preceding the verb or particle by ما (MSA: لَيْسَ، لا، لم).

Smoking

Key Words

صِحّة health	سيجارة (سجائر) cigarette
تدْخين smoking	دُخّان tobacco

Main Idea

Luma tells us about ___.

  a. the culture surrounding the water pipe in Arab countries
  b. general scientific information on the dangers of smoking
  c. Jordanians' smoking habits and their attitudes toward smoking
  d. her personal struggles with smoking

True or False

  1. Luma mentions bad breath among the negative consequences of smoking.
  2. Women nowadays commonly smoke in public.
  3. The government has just recently started introducing smoking bans.
  4. Luma appreciates the water pipe's place in Arab culture.
  5. Luma and her children all smoke.

Multiple Choice

  1. You can commonly find people smoking ___ in Jordan.

      a. in taxis   b.   on buses   c.   in offices   d.   *all of the above*

  2. Many banks and offices ___.

      a. have designated smoking areas for their employees
      b. make their employees smoke across the street
      c. let their employees smoke freely at work
      d. will not hire smokers

  3. In the past, you would see ___.

      a. more people smoking than nowadays   c. even younger children smoking
      b. fewer people smoking than nowadays   d. women smoking in public

  4. Luma refers to the water pipe as ___ and ___.

      a. hookah   b.   shisha   c.   narghile   d.   arghila

  5. Sitting at a café smoking a water pipe for a couple hours, a person will have smoked the equivalent of ___ cigarettes.

      a. four   b.   twenty   c.   two packs of   d.   four packs of

Matching

خاصّةً	all over the country
ناهيكَ عن	as for; when it comes to
يوجد	especially
في جميع أنْحاءِ البِلاد	for; since
لا أحد	God only knows!
أمّا بالنِّسْبة إلى... فـ	I don't know whether...
مُؤَخَّرًا جِدًّا	nobody; no one
ومعَ هذا	not to mention; let alone
تجِد	really; actually
في الحقيقة	still; nonetheless
لا أدْري إذا	there is; there are
اللهُ أعْلم	very recently
مُنْذُ	you (can) find; you see

Text

النّاس، والصّحّة، والجَوّ العامّ... كُلّها تتأثّر مِنَ التّدْخين.	1	People, health, the atmosphere... everything's affected by smoking.
رائِحة الـ... رائِحة الإنْسان وخاصّةً رائِحة فم الإنْسانِ المُدخِّن شَيْءٌ مُزري وغَيْر مُحبِّب.	2	How people smell, and especially how the mouths of people who smoke smell, is a sorry, unfavorable thing.
ناهيكَ عن صِحّة المُدخِّن الّتي تتأثّر تأثُّرًا سِلْبيًّا بِعدد السّجائِر الّتي يستهْلِكُها ويحرقُها في اليَوْم.	3	Not to mention the smoker's health, which is negatively affected by the number of cigarettes he consumes and lights in a day.
التّدْخين في الأرْدُنّ مِثلُهُ مِثلَ أيّ دَوْلة أخْرى في العالم.	4	Smoking in Jordan is like in any other country.
يوجد المُدخِّنين بِشراهة وهُم مُنْتشِرين في جميع أنْحاءِ البِلاد،	5	There are the heavy smokers [spread] all over the country...

في الشَّوارع والمرافق العامّة والتّاكسيات والباصات ومكاتِب الحُكومة والمكاتِب الخاصّة.	6	on the streets, in public places, taxis, buses, government offices, private offices.
وجميع النّاس يعرِفونَ خُطورة التّدخين ومدى تأثيره على الشَّخص الغَيْر مُدخِّن	7	Everybody knows the risks of smoking and the extent of the effects on non-smokers,
ولكن لا أحد يحْترِم هذِهِ المقولة أو الحقيقة العِلْمية المُؤكّدة.	8	but nobody respects this assertion or confirmed scientific fact.
أمّا بالنِّسْبة إلى السيِّدات، فلَيْسَ لدَيْهُنّ الشَّجاعة بعْد للتّدْخين في الأماكِن العامّة	9	As for women, they still lack the courage to smoke in public places,
ولكنّهُم يُدخِّنوا في سيّارتِهنّ الخاصّة والمكاتِب الخاصّة وبُيوتِهنّ طبْعًا.	10*	but they'll smoke in their cars or private offices, and in their homes, of course.
مُؤخّرًا جدًّا تم منْع التّدخين في المرافِقِ العامّة والمكاتِب الحُكوميّة الرّسْمية.	11	Very recently smoking has been banned in public places and official government offices.
وبعْض المطاعِم أصبحت تخصّص قِسْم خاصّ للمُدخِّنين.	12	And some restaurants have begun designating smoking sections.
أمّا المكاتِب الخاصّة والبُنوك مثلًا فهيَ تخصّص مِنطقة مُزرية جدًّا للمُدخِّنينَ مِن مُوظّفيها	13	As for private offices and banks, for example, they designate really miserable areas for the smokers among their staff.
ومعَ هذا لا أحدَ يرْتدِع عنِ التّدْخين أوْ يُخفِّف مِنه.	14	Still, no one is deterred from smoking or smokes less.
في الحقيقة التّدْخين بالزّمن القديم كان يقْتصِر فقط على الكبار مِنَ النّاس	15	Really, in the past, smoking was limited only to adults.
وما كُنْتَ تجِد سائِق تكْسي مثلًا يُدخّن وهُوَ في مجالٍ عمله.	16	You would never see a taxi driver, for example, smoking in his place of work.
كُنْتَ تجِد فقط مُوظّفي الحُكومة هُم الّذينَ يُدخِّنونَ في مكاتِبِهم.	17	You would only see civil servants smoking in their offices.
فالتّدْخين كانَ مِن ضِمْنِ الأشياء الغَيْر ضرورية في حَياةِ الفرْد.	18	And so, smoking wasn't an important part of people's lives.
ولم تكُنْ تجِد سيِّدات مُدخِّنات كثيرات.	19	You wouldn't find many women smoking.
فقط سيِّدات المُجْتمعات المُخْملية مُمْكِن أنْ نقول كُنّ يتمتّعْنَ بهذِهِ المِيزة...لا أدْري إذا كانت هذِهِ مَيزة.	20	Just high-society women, so to speak, enjoyed this privilege...)I don't know(if you can call it a privilege.
أمّا بالنِّسْبة للشيشة أو الأرْجيلة هذِهِ مرض خطير يجْتاح العالم العربي كُلّه	21*	As for the shisha [hookah/water pipe], or arghila, this is a serious malady that has afflicted the entire Arab world.
ولا يخْلو مقْهى أوْ مطْعم مِن تقْديم الأرْجيلة (أوِ الشّيشة) بأنْواعِها ونكهاتِها والتّفنُّن في تقْديمها.	22	There's no café or restaurant that doesn't offer the arghila (or shisha) with all of its varieties and sweet scents and creative way to serve it.
هذِهِ الآفة الخطيرة سبقت وستسْبق قُنْبُلة تْشيرْنوبيل في اِنْتِشار مضارها على الجِنْس البشري.	23	This grave epidemic has surpassed, and will surpass, the Chernobyl "bomb" [explosion]

		in the spread of its detriment to the human race.
وتجِد الفتَيات والسيِّدات قاعدينَ في المقاهي ونازْلين تدْخين رأْس ورأسَيْن في القعْدة.	24*	You find girls and women sitting in cafés absorbed in smoking a bowl or two in one sitting.
رأْس الشّيشة هُوَ عِبارة عن تدْخين عِشْرين سيجارة،	25	A bowl of shisha is equivalent to smoking twenty cigarettes.
يَعْني بِخِلال قعْدة على مدى ساعتَيْن بِكون المُشيِّش أو المُوَرِّجل مُدخِّن مِش أقلّ مِن أرْبع باكيتات سجائر وهُوَ يُغيِّر رأْس الشّيشة.	26	That is, over the course of a two-hour sitting, the shisha-smoker will have smoked four packs of cigarettes by changing out the bowls of shisha.
هذا المَوْضوع موْضوع جِدًّا مُقْرِف وغَيْر حضاري.	27	This situation is really a disgusting, uncivilized situation.
ويجْلِب الأمْراض ولكِن لا أحد يتَّعِظ ولا يُفكِّر بالضّرر.	28	It brings about illnesses, but nobody learns (their lesson) or thinks of the harm.
بدأ... بدأت الحُكومة مُؤخَّرًا جِدًّا بِمنْع بيع الشّيشة في المقاهي،	29	The government has just recently begun to ban the sale of shishas in cafés.
ولكِن ما هُوَ مدى جِدّية هذا المنْع	30	But how serious is this ban?
وهل سيتقبَّل أصْحاب المقاهي المُنْتشِرة في أنْحاء المَمْلكة مِن تطْبيقِها.	31	And will café owners in all corners of the kingdom welcome its implementation?
الله أعْلم.	32	God [only] knows.
بعْد كُلّ الِلي قُلْتُهُ عن الدُّخَان، أحُبّ أن أقول إنّي أُدخِّن أرْبع سجائر فقط في اليَوْم مُنْذُ أرْبعينَ سنة.	33*	After everything I've said about tobacco, I'd like to add that I've smoked just four cigarettes a day for forty years.
ولا أُدخِّن داخِل منْزِلي ولكِن على الشُّرفة خارِج البَيْت	34	I don't smoke in the house, just on the balcony outside the house.
ولا أُدخِّن خارِج منْزِلي أبدًا يعْني لا بِضيافة ولا عِنْدَ السِّتات ولا بالمطاعِم.	35	I don't smoke away from home, that is, on visits (to others' homes), with lady friends, or in restaurants.
وأوْلادي بِدخَّنوا زَيِّي بالضبط، أرْبع سجائر باليَوْم.	36	And my children smoke just like me, four cigarettes a day.
فيارَيْت كُلّ النّاس بتدخّن زَيِّي.	37	If only everyone would smoke like me.
شُكرًا.	38	Thank you.

Notes

*10 Here, the feminine plural ولكِنَّهُنَّ يُدخِّنَّ should have been used. Most dialects, such as Luma's, replace the feminine plural with the masculine plural, and so it is common to see native speakers failing to use the feminine plural correctly.

*21 Picture on the right: shishas lined up outside a restaurant

*24 قاعدينَ should be the feminine plural قاعدات.

*33 Toward the end of this segment, Luma starts to mix MSA with her dialect.

Childhood Memory

Key Words

إِبْرَة syringe   بَيّاع vendor

Main Idea

Walid tells us about a misunderstanding between himself and ___.

   a. a salesman   b.   a doctor   c.   a policeman   d.   his mother

True or False

1. The perfume salesmen had fancy shops with display windows full of beautiful bottles.
2. The incident took place when Walid was about seven years old.
3. Walid had never seen a perfume vendor before.
4. Walid's mother bought a few bottles of perfume.
5. Walid ran all the way home.

Multiple Choice

1. Why would Walid's mother go to Sidon every week?

   a. to visit the doctor   c. to buy groceries
   b. to sell handicrafts   d. *all of the above*

2. Walid seems to feel ___ when he thinks back on the incident.

   a. amused   b.   distraught c.   embarrassed   d.   angry

3. The perfume salesman filled small perfume bottles ___.

   a. by pouring the perfume directly from larger bottles
   b. using a syringe
   c. using a funnel and a spoon
   d. with a strange machine that looked like a coffee maker

4. Walid thought the perfume salesman was trying to ___.

   a. overcharge his mother   c. squirt a little perfume in his hair
   b. inject perfume into his head   d. make him smell like a girl

5. In the end, Walid's mother ___.

   a. gave him a good spanking   c. felt embarrassed that people
   b. made him apologize to the   were laughing
        perfume salesman   d. laughed and laughed

Matching

MSA	LCA	English
أرى	حأَحْكِيْلْكُن	a little; a few
ألم تَرَيْ؟	كِثير مهْضوم	Anyway,...
إلى الـ	أنا وصغير	bottles
بدأتُ	ضيعْتي	Didn't you see?
الّذي، الّتي	ريحة	he wants; she wants
زجاجات	يَلّي	I began
سأحْكي لكُم	باشوف	I found
عِطْر	شِوّي	I see
على كُلِّ حالٍ،	بدُّه، بدُّها	I'm going to tell you
عِنْدما كُنْتُ صغيرًا	أناني	my village
قرْيَتي	تَبييعوهُن	perfume
قليلًا	هال	so that they (can) sell them
لِماذا؟	عكلّ حال،	there
لِيَبيعوها	لَقَيْت	this ___
ماذا حدثَ؟	بلّشْت	to the ___
مُضحِك جِدًّا	هونيك	very funny
هذا الـ هذه الـ	عال	What happened?
هُناكَ	شو صار؟	when I was little
وجدْتُ	ليه؟	who; which; that
يُريدُ، تُريدُ	ما شُفْتي؟	Why?
إلى أينَ يذْهبُ؟	هون	here; at this point
كذلكَ	وهيْك	like that; that way
لكُم	هيْك	so that...
لِكَيْ	مين؟	Where's he going?
من؟	لَوَيْن رايِح؟	who?
هُنا	كُن	you

Answers

Main Idea: a **True or False:** 1. F[6] 2. T[10] 3. T[12] 4. T[14] 5. F[21] **Multiple Choice:** 1. c[5] 2. a[3,38] 3. b[16] 4. b[24] 5. d[25,36]

Matching: حأَحْكِيْلْكُن I'm going to tell you أنا وصغير when I was little عِنْدما كُنْتُ سأحْكي لكُم / كِثير مهْضوم very funny مُضحِك جِدًّا / ضيعْتي my village قرْيَتي / عِطْر perfume ريحة شِوّي a little; a few / أرى I see باشوف / يَلّي who; which; that الّذي، الّتي / صغيرًا

this هـال / لِيَبيعوها so that they (can) sell them تَبيعوهُن / زجاجات bottles أناني / يُريدُ، تُريدُ he wants; she wants بُدّه، بُدّها، بُدّي / قليلًا
to the عـال / هُناك there هونيك / بلَّشت I began بدأتُ / وجدتُ found لقَيْت / على كُلّ حالٍ، ...عـكلّ حالٍ، Anyway, ... هذا الـ هذه الـ ___
here; at this point هُنا هون / أم تَرَيْ؟ Didn't you see? ما شُفتي؟ / لِماذا؟ لِيه؟ Why? / ماذا؟ ماذا حدثَ؟ What happened? شو صار؟ / إلى الـ
you كُنّ / إلى أينَ يذهبُ؟ Where's he going? لوَيْن رايح؟ / من؟ who? مين؟ / كذلكَ like that; that way هَيْك / لِكَيْ so that... وهَيْك كُم

Text

كِلّ إنْسان عنْدُه كِثير ذِكرَيات طُفولة حلوْة،	1	Everyone has a lot of beautiful childhood memories.
منْها الْلي بضحِّك ومنْهُ الْلي بِبكّي.	2*	Some make you laugh and some make you cry.
اليَوم حأحْكيلْكُن قصّة كِثير مهْضومة صارت معي أنا وصغير. هبل ولاد يعْني ههه...	3*	Today, I am going to tell you a really funny story that happened to me when I was child, a mad child, that is... ha-ha.
أنا وصغير تعوّدْنا نْروح كلّ نهار سبت على صَيْدا، أقْرب مدينة لضيعْتي،	4①	When I was a child, we used to go each Saturday to Sidon, the nearest city to my hometown
نِشْتري أغْراض وأكْل للجِمْعة كِلّها.	5	to buy necessities and food for the whole week.
كان فيها شارع للبيّاعين يلّي بِبيعوا ريحة.	6	There was a street there with street-vendors selling perfumes.
تعوّدْنا نعيطلْهُن رجال الريحة.	7	We used to call them "perfume-men".
كانوا يِحْملوا عِلْبة فيها أناني ريحة ويبيعوا هالأناني.	8	They would carry a box with perfume bottles in it, and they would sell these bottles.
أيّام ينْطروا وقْت طويل عالطّريق تَبيعوهُن.	9	Sometimes they would wait on the street for a long time to sell them.
كان تقريبًا عُمْري سبع سِنين، رحْت معَ الماما عالسّوق بِهديك المدينة نْجيب أغْراض.	10	When I was about seven years old, I went to the market in that city with my mom to buy necessities.
ماما راحت على أقْرب بيّاع ريحة تِشْتري مِنُه ريحة.	11	My mother went to the nearest perfume-vendor to buy perfume from him.
كانت أوّل مرّة باشوف فيها بيّاع ريحة.	12	It was the first time I saw a perfume-vendor.
كان طَويل وشعْرُه أبَيَض وعنْدُه دقْن.	13	He was a tall man with a white hair and beard.
صاروا يحْكوا شِوّي وماما صار بدّها تِشْتري أناني ريحة صغار.	14	They talked a little and my mother wanted to buy a few small bottles of perfume.
بيّاع الرّيحة كان معُه أناني كِبار وإبْرة كْبيرة.	15	The perfume-vendor had large bottles of perfume and a big syringe.
صار بِسْتعْمل هالإبْرة تَنْقُل الرّيحة عالأناني الصّغار.	16	He would use that syringe to transfer perfume to the small bottles.
عكِلّ حال، عبّاهُن وخلص.	17	Anyway, he bottled them up and it was all done.
وفجْأة لقَيْت هالرّجال عم يِقْرب علَيّ وحامِل إبْرتُه الكبيرة.	18	Suddenly, I found that man was coming toward me with his big syringe!
صار يِقْرب، يِقْرب، يِقْرب، يِقْرب. يا اللّه...	19	He kept coming closer and closer... Oh my God!

أنا بهاللّحْظة مِثل البرق صُرْت برّة الشارع وبلّشْت ركُض.	20	At that time I rushed out onto street and started to run.
تركْت الماما هونيك وركضْت عالسّيارة.	21	I left my mom there and ran to the car.
بعْد عشر دقايِق تقْريبًا بِتوصِل ماما عالسّيارة.	22	Some ten minutes later, my mother came to the car.
بِتْقولّي: شو صار؟ لَيْه ركضْت بِسُرْعة وتركْتْني هونيك؟	23	She said, "What happened? Why did you run off and leave me there?"
قُلْتلْها: ما شُفْتي رِجال الرّيحة كان بدُّه يِشكّ برْأسي للإبْرة.	24*	I said, "Didn't you see? The perfume-man wanted to inject me in my head!"
هون بلّشت الماما بالضحْك بِصَوْت عالي وصارت تقولّي:	25	Then my mother began to laugh out loud and said,
لأ، ما كان جاي يِعْملّك إبْرة.	26	"He wasn't coming to inject you.
بسّ كان بدُّه يِرْشلك شِوّية ريحة وهَيْك ريحة شعْرك بِتصير حلْوة،	27	He just wanted to spray a little perfume on you so your hair would smell nice,
وإنْتَ افْتكرْت جاي يِعْملّك إبْرة برأسك.	28	and you thought he wanted to inject you in your head, ha!"
عن جدّ فكرْت هَيْك بوقْتها.	29	I really thought that at the time.
كِنْت خاف مِن شكّة الإبْرة	30	I was afraid of the jab of the syringe.
وحتى لَوْ كِنْت مريض ولازِم أعْمل إبْرة، خِفْت على رأْسي.	31	Even if I got ill and needed an injection, I worried about my head.
يا الله شو كانت حلْوة هالأيّام.	32	My god, how beautiful were those days!
بعْدْني كِلّ ما أنْزل على صَيْدا وعلى هالسّوق، باتْذكّر هالّحْظة، كيف صُرْت أرْكُض مِثل الأخْوَت	33	Whenever I go to Sidon and to that street, I still remember that moment and how I was running like a fool,
والنّاس تِقول: شو باه الولد؟	34	and people were shouting, "What's wrong with this child?
مِن مين خايِف وهِرْبان؟ ولَوَيْن رايِح؟	35	Who is he scared of, running away? And where is he going?"
وكيف صارت الماما تِضْحك و تِضْحك و تقولّي: كِنْت مِثل الأخْوَت راكِض عالطّريق.	36	And how my mother was laughing and laughing and told me, "You were running down the street like a fool."
إن شاء اللة تْكون عجبتْكُن قُصْتي	37	I hope you like my story.
وإذا صارت معكُن، ما تْخافوا مِثلي. ههه...	38	And if it happens with any of you, do not get scared like me. Ha-ha.

Notes

*2 Levantine Arabic, as many other dialects of Arabic, adds the prefix بـ b- to mark the present tense. The 3rd person masculine prefix يـ is usually dropped when the present tense prefix بِـ is added.

*3 The future tense is formed by adding حَـ to the imperfect verb (MSA: سـ سَوْفَ).

*24 The negative is formed by preceding the verb or particle by ما (MSA: لَيْسَ، لا، م).

ⓘ4 wikipedia.org/wiki/Sidon

Transportation

Key Words

وَسائِل النّقْل transportation	درّاجة هَوائية bicycle	سيّارة أُجْرة taxi
سيّارة خاصّة personal car	قِطار train	

Main Idea

a. Atheer discusses forms of transportation in his hometown.
b. Atheer compares forms of transportation in Baghdad and Basra.
c. Atheer discusses forms of transportation in Iraq.
d. Atheer compares forms of transportation in Iraq and the U.S.

True or False

1. In Iraq, transportation networks are all state-owned.
2. Most students use mini-buses.
3. You can take a taxi for hundreds of kilometers for under $50.
4. It takes roughly two hours by bus from Basra to Baghdad.
5. Atheer believes that domestic flights should be cheaper than they are.

Multiple Choice

1. Bicycles are **not** always an ideal way to get around in Basra because of ___.

    a. poor road conditions
    b. the hot climate
    c. frequent violence in the streets
    d. the hilly terrain

2. It costs almost $180 for a ___.

    a. round-trip flight between Basra and Erbil
    b. round-trip flight between Basra and Baghdad
    c. one-way flight from Basra to Baghdad
    d. one-way flight from Erbil to Sulaymaniyah

3. Atheer recommends ___ if traveling from Basra to northern Iraq.

    a. flying   b. driving   c. taking a bus   d. taking the train

4. Atheer says train service ___.

    a. has been a reliable means of transportation for decades
    b. is too expensive for most people
    c. is only available in northern Iraq
    d. was suspended until recently

5. To get around Basra, Atheer usually ___.

    a. takes taxis   b. takes mini-buses   c. drives his own car   d. rides a bicycle

Matching

عُمومًا	approximately; around
مِن قِبَلِ	as for; when it comes to
بِالنِّسْبة لِـ	by
بقية الـ	either... or
أكْثر الـ	for a period of time
أمّا أنْ... أوْ...	generally; in general
في بعْض الأحْيان	in order to...; so that...
رَيْثَما	instead of
تقْريبًا	it is better to...
إلى حدٍّ كبير	it is necessary to...; it is essential that...
مِنَ الأفْضل أنْ	most; most of the
بدلًا مِن	recently; lately
مُؤَخَّرًا	sometimes
لِفتْرة مِنَ الزّمن	the rest of
مِنَ الضُّروري أنْ	to a large extent
لِكَيْ	until

Answers

Main Idea: c **True or False:** 1. F[4] 2. T[5] 3. T[10] 4. F[13] 5. T[19] **Multiple Choice:** 1. b[6] 2. b[11-12] 3. a[15-16] 4. d[17] 5. c[5]

Matching: عُمومًا generally; in general / مِن قِبَلِ by / بِالنِّسْبة لِـ as for; when it comes to / بقية الـ the rest of / أكْثر الـ most; most of the / أمّا أنْ... أوْ... either... or... / في بعْض الأحْيان sometimes / رَيْثَما until / تقْريبًا approximately; around / إلى حدٍّ كبير to a large extent / مِنَ الأفْضل أنْ it is better to... / بدلًا مِن instead of / مُؤَخَّرًا recently; lately / لِفتْرة مِنَ الزّمن for a period of time / مِنَ الضُّروري أنْ it is necessary to...; it is essential that... / لِكَيْ in order to...; so that...

Text

مَرْحَبًا. أنا اِسْمي أثير.	1	Hello. My name is Atheer,
واليَوْم سنتكلّم عن وسائِل النَّقْل بالعراق.	2	and today we will talk about transportation in Iraq.
عُمومًا على المُسْتَوَى الشَّخْصي فأكْثر النّاس تسْتعْمِل سيّاراتْها الخاصّة ولَيْسَ لدَيْنا شبكة مُواصلات حُكومية.	3	Generally, on a personal level most people use their own cars; we do not have a government [i.e. public] transportation network.
نَعم، لدَيْنا شبكة مُواصلات ولكِنّها عِبارة عن أفْراد وتُدار مِن قِبلِ الحُكومة ولكِنْ لَيْسَ لدَيْنا شبكة مُواصلات حُكومية.	4	True, we have a transportation network, but it is privately owned and is managed by the government, but we do not have a government transportation network.
بالنِّسْبة للتّنقُّلات داخِل المدينة أنا أسْتعْمِل سيّارتي الخاصّة كما بقية النّاس وأكْثر الطُّلّاب يسْتعْمِلونَ الباصات الصغيرة.	5	For movements within the city, I use my own car, like the rest of the people [do]. Most students use mini-buses.
أمّا بالنِّسْبة لاِسْتعْمال الدَّرّاجات الهَوائية فأنّهُ مُقْتصِر على أوْقات مُعيّنة مِنَ السّنة بِسبب مناخ البصْرة الحارّ.	6	As for the use of bicycles, it is limited to certain times of the year due to the hot climate of Basra.
بالنِّسْبة للتّنقِلات بَيْنَ المُحافظات فهُنالِكَ خِيارَيْن:	7	For movements between the provinces there are two choices:
أمّا أنْ تذهب بِسيّارتِكَ الخاصّة أوْ تسْتقِلّ سيّارات الأُجْرة والّتي عِبارة عن سيّارات صالون أوْ فان مُكيّفة	8	either you go in your own car or take taxis, which is a sedan or air-conditioned van,
وقد تحْتَوِي على شاشات لِعرْض الفيدِيُو في بعْض الأحْيان.	9	which may contain screens to display videos [movies] in some cases.
هذا بالنِّسْبة للمُدُنِ القريبة مِنَ البصْرة يعْني على بُعْد ثلاثِمائة كيلو وقد تكلّفُكَ الأُجْرة ما يُعادِل أرْبعين دولارا.	10	This is for cities near Basra, that is, three hundred kilometers away, and the fare will cost you the equivalent of forty dollars.
أمّا إذا أردْتَ أنْ تذهب إلى بغْداد فالخِيارات تكون أكْثر فبالإضافة إلى الخِيارات أدْناه.	11*	But if you want to go to Baghdad there are more choices in addition to the options below.
مُمْكِنُكَ أنْ تأخُذَ الباص والّذي يأخُذ وقْت... رَيْثَما يمْتلِئ أوْ مُمْكِنُكَ أنْ تأخُذ الطّيّارة والّتي قد تُكلِّفُكَ تقْريبًا مائةٌ وثمانونَ دولار ذهابًا وإيابًا.	12	You can take a bus, which takes time... until it fills up [with people] or you can take the plane, which may cost you almost one hundred and eighty dollars round trip.
الشَّيْء الجيّد هُنا أنّكَ تخْتصِر الوقْت إلى حدٍّ كبير فالرَّحْلة إلى بغْداد تأخُذ تقْريبًا ثماني ساعاتٍ	13	The good thing here is that you shorten the time to a large extent, as the journey to Baghdad takes roughly eight hours,
أمّا بالطّيّارة تخْتصِر إلى ساعتَيْنِ أوْ ساعةٍ ونِصْف، إضافةً إلى الأمان وتعب الطّريق الّذي ستتخلّص مِنهُ.	14	but by plane it is shortened to two hours or an hour and a half, in addition to safety and road fatigue that you will have done away with.
أيْضًا هذا الخِيار هُوَ المُرجّح إذا كُنْتَ مُسافِرًا إلى شمال العِراق إلى أرْبيل أوْ السُّلَيْمانية مثلًا،	15	This option is also likely if you are traveling to northern Iraq to Erbil or Sulaymaniyah, for example;

فمِنَ الأفْضل أنْ تأخُذَ الطّائِرة بدلًا مِنَ السَّيّارة الّتي ستأخُذ اثْنا... اثْنا عشَرَ ساعةً لتصِلَ إلى هُناك.	16*	it is better to take the plane instead of the car, which will take twelve hours to reach there.
ومُؤخَّرًا بد... بدأت وِزارة النّقْل العِراقية بتفْعيل خُطوطِ القِطارات بَيْنَ البصْرة وبغْداد وبقية المُحافظات الّتي توقّفت لِفتْرة مِنَ الزّمن.	17	Recently, Iraq's ministry of transportation has begun to activate the train lines between Basra and Baghdad and other provinces, which had stopped for a period of time.
أعْتقِد أنّهُ مِنَ الضّروري أنْ تكون هُناك تنْمية في أكْثر مِنَ اتّجاه في وسائطِ النّقْل أيْ أنْ يتِمَّ الاهْتِمام بالوسائِل مُنْخفِضة الكُلْفة مِثلَ القِطارات وأنْظِمة الباصات،	18	I think it's essential that there be development in more than one direction in transport, that is, that interest be taken in low-cost means of transportation such as trains and bus systems,
وأيْضًا يجِبُ الحِرْص على تخْفيض أجور الطَّيَران الدّاخِلي لِكَيْ يُصْبِحَ مُتاحًا لِلنّاس.	19	and also care must be taken to reduce the fares for domestic flights to become [more] accessible to the people.
خِبرتي معَ النّقْل أكْثرها بقيادة سيّارتي الخاصّة إلى المكان الّذي أنْوي الذّهاب إلَيْه.	20	Most of my experience with transportation has been driving my own car to the place where I intend to go.
وقد يحْدُثُ أنْ آخُذ سيّارة أجْرة على الأقلّ لِكَيْ أتجنَّب تعب الطّريق ولِكَيْ يسْنحَ لي الوقْت بالنّوْم أو القِراءة بالطّريق.	21	And sometimes I at least take a taxi so I [can] avoid road fatigue and to allow me time to sleep or read on the journey.

Notes

*11 Atheer meant to say أعْلاه *above*, not أدْناه *below*.

*16 إثْنا عشَرَ ساعةً should actually be اثْنتَيْ عشرةً ساعةً.

Clothing

Key Words

لبْسة clothing   عُرْيان naked; *here:* provocative(ly), lewd, racy

Main Idea

a. Lilia describes Tunisians' attitudes toward clothing and what they think is appropriate.

b. Tunisia is more conservative when it comes to women's dress than most Arab countries.

c. Lilia describes traditional costumes worn on weddings and other special occasions.

d. Lilia compares Tunisian attitudes toward clothing to those in Egypt and other Arab countries.

True or False

1. Most of Lilia's friends wear the hijab.

2. Most young people in Tunisia wear Western style clothes.

3. The traditional Tunisian bridal dress is very conservative.

4. In Tunisian culture, one's appearance is indicative of one's financial status.

5. Lilia pities the poor who cannot afford to buy nice clothes.

Multiple Choice

1. In Tunisia, religion ___.

   a. plays little or no role in what most people wear these days

   b. still dictates some restrictions on modesty, especially for women

   c. deters most people from wearing Western style clothes

   d. only influences what people wear in the countryside

2. Lilia mentions that the "phenomenon of piety", i.e. wearing the hijab, is most common among ___.

   a. the poor   b. the elderly   c. women in the countryside   d. religious fanatics

3. If a Tunisian woman wears an outfit that shows too much skin, ___.

   a. she may be arrested   c. men will likely harass her
   b. her family may discipline or   d. people will assume she is a
      disown her   foreigner

4. Lilia sees ___ as a contradiction to what are taught to be Tunisian society's values.

   a. high heels and skirts   c. men wearing shorts
   b. the hijab   d. the traditional wedding dress

5. Which of the following is **not** true?

   a. Tunisians value dressing nicely very deeply.

   b. Lilia feels a person should never be measured in terms of their clothes.

   c. Lilia implies that the elderly are out of touch and backward in their way of thinking.

   d. Lilia implies that the youth of the upper class are shallow and judgmental.

Matching

MSA	TCA	English
أَنْ	كيما	above all
أَوْ	برْشا	beautiful; nice
جِدًّا	سُغْتو	because
جميل	باش	clothes
الَّذي، الَّتي	مْعرِّس	for example
قَبْلَ كُلِّ شَيْءٍ	مْتاع	from what
لا نسْتطيعُ	مُش	(in order) to
لِأَنَّ	على خاطِر	like
لِذلِكَ	باغ أَكْزامْبْل	married
لَيْسَ	اِلّي	not
مُتزوِّج	ولّا	of
مِثْل	دُونْك	or
مثلًا	مِزْيان	otherwise
ملابِس	مناش	so; thus
مِمّا	ما نْنجْموش	very
وإلّا	دْبش	we can't
(no translation)	سينون	who; which; that
إذا كُنْتَ	زادة	also; too
إنْسان (ناس)	علّاخِر	always
أَيْضًا	باهي	extremely
جَيِّد	شنُوّ	good
دائمًا	عبد (عباد)	he shouldn't
كثيرًا	كانك	if you
لِلْغاية	ما لازْموش	just
ماذا	جوسْت	person (people)
مُجَرّد	ديما	really; a lot
يجِبُ ألّا	ياسر	what

Answers

Main Idea: a **True or False:** 1. F[7] 2. T[9] 3. F[23] 4. T[27-29] 5. F[37,41] **Multiple Choice:** 1. b[3] 2. b[8] 3. c[13-15] 4. d[20,23] 5. c[27,32-34,38] **Matching:** كيما like / برْشا / مِثْل very جِدًّا / سُغْتو above all قَبْلَ كُلِّ شَيْءٍ / باش (in order) to أَنْ / مْعرِّس married مُتزوِّج / مْتاع of /

لِذلِكَ / دُونَكْ so; thus / وَلَّا / الَّذِي، الَّتِي who; which; that / مَثَلًا / اِللِّي for example / باغ أَكْزامْبُل / لِأَنَّ because / عَلى خاطِر / لَيْسَ مُش not
زادة / وِإلَّا otherwise / سينون / مَلابِس / دْبش clothes / لا نَسْتطيعُ we can't / ما نْنَجّموش / مناش / جَميل beautiful; nice / مِزْيان /
also; too / أَيْضًا / عَلآخِر extremely / لِلغايَة / باهي good / جَيّد / شُؤُو what / ماذا / عبد (عباد) person (people) / إنْسان (ناس) كانك if you / إذا
really; a lot / كَثيرًا / ياسر / دائِمًا always / دِيما / مُجَرّد just / جوسْت / يَجِبُ أَلَّا / ما لازموش he shouldn't / كُنْتَ

Text

اللِّبْسة في بِلاد عربية مُسْلِمة كيما بِلادي تونس، هِيَ حاجة مهِمّة برْشا.	1	Clothes, in a Muslim Arab country, like mine, are of great importance,
فـ... عاداتْنا وتقاليدْنا وسُغْتو (surtout) دينّا ما يِسْمحولْناش باش نِلْبْسُو اِللِّي يجي، خاصّةً بِالنِّسْبة لِلبْنات.	2*	as our customs and traditions, and above all our religion do not allow us to wear just whatever, especially when it comes to girls.
بِالنِّسْبة لِلحِجاب، صْحيح يُعْتْبر فرْض في الدِّين مْتاعْنا،	3	As for the hijab, it is true that it is imposed by our religion.
ولكِن مُش البْناتْ الكُلّ بِلْبْسوه.	4	However, not all girls wear it.
هُنا البْناتْ ااا... تْحِسّْهُمْ مِتْحرّرين أكْثر مِن البُلْدان المُسْلِمة الأُخْرى،	5	Here, girls uh... are more liberal than those in any other Muslim country,
عْلى خاطِر في تونس أكْثر العايِلات ما... ما تُفْرُضْش الحِجاب على بناتْها.	6	because in Tunisia, most families don't... don't impose the hijab on their daughters.
آنا باغ أَكْزامْبُل (par exemple) عِنْدي تقْريبًا عْلى كلّ عشرة صحْبات صاحْبة واحْدة مِتْحَجْبة، اِللِّي هِيَ نِسْبة صغيرة برْشا.	7	For example, I have approximately one friend in ten who wears a hijab, which is a very small number.
ااا... ظاهرة التديّن نِلْقاوْها الأكْثرِيّة عِند النِّساء الكِبار، ولا المْعرّسين ولا اِللّي عِنْدهُم صْغار.	8	Uh... the phenomenon of piety [i.e. wearing hijab] is most common among old ladies, or married ones or mothers [lit. those who have young ones].
دونْك (donc) أغْلبِيّة الشْباب هُنا يِلْبِسوا عْلى الطَّريقة الغرْبية. معْناها دْجينات، ااا... دا تي شورْت (des T-shirts)، كاسْكِتات، دا جيب (des jupes) بِالنِّسْبة لِلبْنات.	9	So, most young people here dress in Western style, meaning jeans, t-shirts, caps, skirts for the girls.
ااا... وقْت اِللِّي نُخْرجو نسْهرو مثَلًا.. نِلْبسو الأكْثرِيّة دا غوب (des robes) مِزْيانين ودا تالون (talons).	10*	Uh... when we go partying, most of the time we wear nice dresses and high heels.
حاسيلو نْحُطّو الحَطّة.	11	In brief, we go out dressed up.
ولكِن هذا ما يْمْنعْش إنّه أَحْنا البْنات مناش أحْرار برْشا في لبْسْتنا كَيْ نُخْرْجو لِلشّارع.	12	However, that doesn't mean we girls are very free in our clothing when we go out.
مثَلًا ما نْنَجّموش نِلْبسو العرْيان.	13	For instance, we can't dress showing too much skin,
وما نْنَجّموش نِلْبسو دْبش يِجْلب الإنْتِباه،	14	or wear an outfit that attracts attention.
سينون (sinon) نوليْوْ عُرْضة لِلمشاكِل والقلق مِن قِبَّل الرّجال.	15	Otherwise, we would be exposed to problems and disturbance from men.

أمّا في المُؤسّسات العُمومية خاصّة المُؤسّسات التّربَوية، الواحِد لازمُه زادة يِلبِس لبْسة مِحتَرْمة علّاخِر.	16	Moreover, in public institutions, and in particular educational institutions, one should also be very respectfully-clad.
الأولاد مثلاً ما لازِمهُمْش يِلبِسوا كسكاتات ولّا شورتُوات .	17	Males for instance shouldn't wear caps or shorts,
والبِنات مِن المُستحسِن إنّهُم ما يِلبِسوش العُريان.	18	and as for the girls, it is preferable that they avoid wearing 'lewd' clothes.
ااه... في النُّقطة هذي آنا شخْصيًا نِلاحظ تناقُض كبير بُرشا لِتوّا لا فُهِمْتو.	19	Uh... at this point, I personally have noticed a great contradiction which I still don't understand.
فمِن ناحْية أحْنا البْنات يقولولْنا الكِبار الّي مِش باهي نُخْرُجو لابْسين العرْية	20	On one hand, we girls are always told by the elderly that it is not okay that we go out showing too much skin
والّي الدّبش العرْيان، ما يِمَتِّلْش هُويّتْنا وعاداتْنا.	21	or that we dress provocatively, which do not represent our identity or customs,
والّي هالنّوْع مْتاع الحْوايِج هُوَ دخيل على قِيَمْنا أتْسَتَغا (et cétéra).	22	and that this kind of clothing is alien to our values, etc.
وْفي نفْس الوقت نشوفو إنّه اللّبسة التّقْليدية التّونْسية الّي تْوارثْناها أجْيال وْراء أجْيال هيَ لبْسة عرْيانة نوْعًا ما.	23	But at the same time, we can see that the Tunisian traditional dress, that we have inherited generation after generation, is also rather risqué.
ااه... اللّبسة هذي العروسة التّونْسية لازِم تِلبْسها نْهارة عرْسها، في حْضور الرّجال زادة،	24	Uh... The Tunisian bride must wear this dress on her wedding day, even in front of males.
وهيَ لبْسة مِزْيانة بُرشا ولكِن عرْيانة!	25	It is indeed a nice dress but racy, as well.
دونْك (donc) هْنا ما فهِمْتِش شْنوّ الأصل وشْنوّ الدخيل؟	26	So, here I can't understand what is original and what is foreign.
في بْلادي اللّبسة عِنْدها قيمتْها الاِجْتماعية،	27	In my country, clothes have a social value,
العْباد ياسر يِقيّموا بعْضهُم بالدّبش الّي لابْسينُه،	28	and many people assess each other through the kind of clothes they are wearing.
وهيأة العبد تِخلّينا نْنجّمو نْطلّعو المُستوى المادّي مْتاعُه.	29	And a person's appearance enables us to infer their financial status.
ااه... كانك لابِس بالكدا وحاطِط الحطّة، أهوْكا... يِحْتَرْموك ويِقدّروك. ويِبجْلوك	30	Uh... If you are well-dressed, then people will respect you and value you, and privilege you
على خاطِرك ظاهِر مالطّبْقة العُليا.	31	because you seem to belong to the upper class.
وكانك مهِنتِل وماكْش كادِد روحك، ااه... هْنا يْنجّمو يْحقْروك ويْطقّيوك!	32	And if you are not dressed up, uh... here they might belittle you and ignore you!
وهذي فِكرة سطْحية ومتْخلّفة،	33	And this is a shallow and backward way of thinking,
عْلى خاطِر الإنْسان ما لازْموش يِتْقاس بِدبْشُه.	34	because a person should never be measured in terms of his clothes.
تي بعْد ساعات، تِنجّم توصل ادبّر خدْمة جوسْت (juste) عْلى خاطِرك لابِس بالكُدا!	35	Sometimes, you can even get a job just because you're well-clad!

أمّا الشّباب مالطّبقة العُليا هاذوكُم عادْ مذابيهم ديما يُخْرُجو كان في أحْلى وأضْخم لبْسة،	36	When it comes to the youth of the upper class, they are always in their nicest and most elegant outfits.
وْما يِلْبِسو كان السّينيا. حاسيلو تْقولْش علَيْهُم عامْلين سِباق!	37	They wear only brand clothes, (in brief) as if they were in a race!
حكاياتْهُم الكُلّ: هاو شوف هذاكا شِ لبِس	38	All they talk about is, "Look at what he is wearing."
وهاو شوف السّاك (sac) مُتاع هذيكا مْحلاة	39	"Look at her nice bag."
والسْبادْري هذاكا يِعْمل بْستّميات دينار.	40	"Look at these trainers. They're about 600 dinars."
حاسيلو مْساكِن اِلْي ما عنْدهُمْش فْلوس باش يِشْريو دبش مِزْيان.	41	"How poor are those who cannot afford to buy nice clothes."

Notes

*2 The negative is formed by sandwiching a verb (or particle) with ما....ش. A distinguishing feature of Tunisian Arabic is the usage of many French words, especially nouns. See also Lilia's self-introduction in book 1, segment 5.

*10 The 1st person singular imperfect prefix is نـ (MSA: أ). This may look like the 1st person plural imperfect prefix of MSA, but in Tunisian Arabic this would also take the suffix ـو: نُسْكُن *I live*; نُسْكْنو *we live*

Daily Routines

Key Words

سِرْقة theft   حطب wood

Main Idea

Abdulkarem talks about ___.

  a. his father's daily routine
  b. an imam's daily routine
  c. his daily routine these days
  d. his daily routine as a child

True or False

  1. Abdulkarem would go to the mosque with his father early in the morning.
  2. Abdulkarem would prepare breakfast for himself and his siblings.
  3. Mosques would close outside of prayer times.
  4. The imam entrusted Abdulkarem and his friends to keep an eye on the mosque.
  5. Abdulkarem feels his routines as a child were typical.

Multiple Choice

  1. Which of the following does Abulkarem not mention?

      a. cleaning his room   c. preparing breakfast
      b. going to the mosque   d. storing wood

  2. Abdulkarem would buy ___ from the market for 10 buqsha.

      a. rice   b. beans   c. coffee   d. wood

  3. Abdulkarem had ___.

      a. one brother and three sisters   c. three brothers and two sisters
      b. two brothers and three sisters   d. three brothers and one sister

  4. What happened one day when Abdulkarem and his friend left the mosque when they were supposed to be keeping an eye on it?

      a. Children vandalized it.   c. It was robbed.
      b. It caught on fire.   d. *all of the above*

  5. The Yemeni word for *a place to store wood* is ___.

      a. حرّ ḥarr   b. بُقْشة buqšaᵗ   c. جمنة jamanaᵗ   d. حطب ḥaṭab

Matching

عِنْدما	after that; afterward
ثُمَّ	because; since; as
عِبارة عن	consists of
بعْدَ ذلك	is called
وحَيْث أنَّ	so that; in order to
عادةً	some
يُسمّى	then
لِكَيْ	usually
بعْض مِن الـ	when

Answers

Main Idea: d **True or False:** 1. T[2-3] 2. F[11-12] 3. T[17] 4. T[19] 5. T[31] **Multiple Choice:** 1. a[3,4,29] 2. b[8-9] 3. a[12] 4. c[22] 5. a[29]

Matching: عِنْدما when / ثُمَّ then / عِبارة عن consists of / بعْدَ ذلك after that; afterward / وحَيْث أنَّ because; since; as / عادةً usually / يُسمّى is called / لِكَيْ so that; in order to / بعْض مِن الـ some

Text

في حَيَاة كُلِّ إنْسان برْنامج مُحدّد ياا... يسْتخْدِمُهُ مِنَ الصّباح الباكِر حتّى عَوْدتِهِ إلى البَيْت إلى المزاء... في المساء.	1	In the life of every person, there's a routine uh... that he has from early morning until he gets back home in the ebning... evening.
أنا تعَوّدْت عِنْدما أصحو مِنَ الصّباح الباكِر أنْ أسْتَيْقِظ في الفجْر	2	When I'd wake up in the morning, I'd get up at dawn
وأذْهبُ مع والِدي إلى الجامِع المُجاوِر لنا فنقوم بأداء صلاة الفجْر ثُمَّ نعود إلى المنْزِل.	3	and go with my father to the mosque nearby to perform the dawn prayer, and then we'd go home.
وكُنْتُ مُتعوّد وأنا صغير أنْ أُحضّر لِوالِدي الفُطور	4	When I was young, I used to prepare breakfast for my dad,
وكانَ هذا الفُطور عِبارة عن قهْوة و... وعن اااه... أكْلة شعْبيّة تُسمّى المُطيط.	5①	and this would consist of coffee and... of uh... a local dish called "muṭayṭ".
وكانَ والِدي يُحِبّ أنْ أعْمل له أنا القهْوة	6	My father liked me to make him coffee,
وكُنْت اااه... أستخْدِم للقهْوة اااه... إناء مِنَ الفخّار يُسمّى الجمنة.	7	and I'd... use clay jars called "jamanaᵗ" for the coffee.
و... بعْدَ ذلك أذْهبُ لِشراء الفول مِنَ السّوق والفول يتِمّ تجْهيزُهُ وإعْدادُهُ في السّوق	8	And... after that I'd go to buy beans from the market, and the beans were prepared [there] at the market.

وأذهبُ لِشِرائِه بِحَوَالي عَشرةٌ... عَشرة بُقش في هذا الأيّام،	9①*	I'd go buy them for about ten... ten buqsha in those days,
أيْ ما يوازي الاا... في هذه الأيّام الاا... رُبْع رِيال بالمَعنى الدّارِج الآن وحَيْث أنّ رِيال مائة فِلْس.	10	which is equivalent to what is... nowadays... a quarter of a rial in modern terms, a rial being one hundred fils.
و... بَعْدَ أنْ أشتري الفول، أرْجِع إلى البَيْت وأعطيْه لِوالِدَتي	11	And... after I bought the beans, I'd go back home and give them to my mom,
الّتي تقوم بِتَجهيز الـ... الصَّبوح، أوْ الفُطور، لي ولِإخوَتي، وعدَدُنا خمسة، ثلاث بنـ... ثلـ... الااه... ثلاثُ بنات واثْنَيْن أوْلاد.	12	who was preparing ṣabūḥ, or breakfast, for me and my siblings. There were five of us, three g... thr... uh... three girls and two boys.
وبعْدَ الفُطور أخُذ حقيبةَ المدرسة وأذهبُ إلى المدرسة.	13	After breakfast, I'd take my school bag and go to school.
وفي المدرسة يتِمّ الاا... الدِّراسة ونحْصُل على الرّاحة حَيْثُ نلعبُ فيها كُرةَ القدم في المدرسة	14	At school, we had lessons, and then we got a break, during which we'd play soccer at school,
وفي الظُّهر نعود إلى المنزِل. ثُمّ يتِمّ الصّلاة وتناوُل الغداء.	15	and in the afternoon we'd go back home. Then we'd pray and have lunch.
ونقْضي فترة الظُّهر في مُذاكرة الدُّروس ومِنَ الأشياء اللّطيفة أنّنا كُنّا نُذاكِر الدُّروس في أحد المساجد القريبة مِن بَيْتِنا	16	We'd spend the afternoons studying. And what was nice was that we'd study at one of the mosques near our house.
و... عادة يتِمّ فتْح المساجِد في وقْت الصّلاة ويتِمّ أغْلاقُها بعْدَ أنْ يتِمّ أداء الصّلاة	17	And... mosques would usually open for prayers and then close after prayers.
وكانَ مسؤُول الجامِع الّذي يُسمّى عِنْدنا باللّهجة المحلّية سُنيدار الجامِع	18	The person responsible for the mosque, whom we call in our local dialect 'sunaydār' of the mosque,
يعْني مسؤُول الجامِع يالا... يوكِلُنا أوْ يرْكن علَيْنا بأنْ نقوم بالمُحافظة أوْ الااه... على الـ... المسْجِد و... على الانْتِباه علَيْه مِن أيّ تلاعُب أوْ اللعِب فيه مِن الأطْفال الصِّغار أوْ أيّ سِرْقة تحْصل	19	that is, 'guardian of the mosque' would entrust us, or put us in charge, of uh... watching the mosque... being on the alert against any kids messing around or playing or any theft that [might] occur.
ففي أحد الأيّام وعنْدما كُنّا نُذاكِر الاا... اسْتمرّيْنا في المُذاكرة إلى بعْدَ العصر بعْدَ صلاة العصر	20*	So, one day we were studying uh... we kept studying until afternoon, until after the afternoon prayer.
فخرجْتُ أنا وزميلي إلى البَيْت لِكَيْ نأخُذ بعْض مِن الأكْل وعُدْنا إلى الجامِع	21	My friend and I went home to get some food, and returned to the mosque.
وقد تمّ سِرْقة الأنْوار الكهْربائية أوْ اللمْبات الكهْربائية مِنَ المسْجِد.	22	The electric lights, or electric lamps, had been stolen.
قام بِه اللُّصوص الّذي عِنْدنا في هذلِك الزّمان تعوّدوا على سِرقة المساجِد	23	The thieves that did this would rob mosques in those days
نتيجةً للظُّروف السَّيِّئة وحالة الفقْر الّتي كانت مَوْجودة في المُجْتمع.	24	because of the bad circumstances and state of poverty that was present in society.

فخُفْنا وكَيْفَ نُواجِهَ الـ... القَيِّم... القَيِّم على المَسْجِد وماذا نقول لهُ	25	We were afraid and how would we face the... the guardian uh... the guardian of the mosque and what would we say to him?
وخُفْنا أيْضًا بأنْ يتِمّ الشّكْوى إلى والِدي وكان ذلك مَوْقِف يعْني مُزْعِج بالنِّسْبة لي ولا زُلْت أتذكّرُهُ حتّى الآن.	26	And we were also afraid he would complain to my father. That situation was, you know, distressing for me, and I still remember it even now.
و... هُناك أيْضًا في البُرْنامج اليَوْمي لِحَياتِنا اليَوْمية أعْمال مَنْزِلية في البَيْت	27	And... in the daily routine of our daily lives, there are also household chores around the house,
حَيْث الوالِد... والِدي عِنْدما يقوم بِشِراء الحطب، نقوم بإنْزالِهِ مِنَ السّـ... مِنَ الـ... مِنَ السّيارة	28	as the father... my father would buy wood, and we'd unload it from the c... from the... from the car.
وإدْخاله إلى ما يُسَمّى عِندنا الحرّ أوْ المكان الّتي... الّذي يتِمّ تخْزين الحطب فيه	29	And we'd put it into what we call a "ḥarr", or a place that... that is for storing wood in.
وهذِهِ بعْضًا مِنَ الـ... اااه... الأعْمال الّتي نقومُ بِها	30	And these are some of the uh... the chores that we do,
و... أعْتقِد بأنّها يعْني روتينية اااه... تكاد تكون مُتشابِهة مِن بَيْت إلى بَيْت ومِن أُسْرة إلى أُسْرة وشُكْرًا.	31	and... I think that they're routine and practically identical from house to house and family to family. Thank you.

Notes

ⓘ5 Recipe for and photos of المُطَيّت: **bit.ly/12plVoQ**

ⓘ9 Wikipedia: **wikipedia.org/wiki/Yemeni_buqsha**

*9 هذاك is Yemeni dialect for تِلْك.

*20 اِسْتمرّنا should actually be اِسْتمرّيْنا in MSA.

Focus

Although this segment is in MSA, Abdulkarem mentions several Yemeni words. Let's see how many words you've picked up. Match these words to their descriptions below.

المُطيط	guardian of a mosque
جمنة	clay coffee pot
بُقْشة، بُقش	place to store firewood
سُنيدار	a local dish
حرّ	former Yemeni monetary unit

Answers: المُطيط a local dish / جمنة clay coffee pot / بُقْشة، بُقش former Yemeni monetary unit / سُنيدار guardian of a mosque / حرّ place to store firewood

Education

Key Words

إعْدادي preparatory	الصَّيْدلة pharmacology	الطِبّ (study of) medicine
التمْريض nursing	الهنْدسة engineering	التّجارة commerce

Main Idea

    a. Islam agrees with a prevalent view on education in his society.

    b. Islam disagrees with a prevalent view on education in his society.

    c. Islam explains the educational system in Egypt.

    d. Islam compares the educational systems in Egypt and Saudi Arabia.

True or False

    1. It is apparent whether a child will be a successful student by the end of his first year of primary school.

    2. People view one's level of education as indicative of social position.

    3. Engineering and commerce are the two most prestigious faculties in Egyptian society.

    4. Over 90% of students aim to get into one of the two most prestigious faculties.

    5. Islam feels his parents pushed him to study engineering, when he really wanted to study nursing.

Multiple Choice

    1. If a student is naughty and not a good student, Islam blames ___.

        a. his parents   c. both his parents and teachers

        b. his teachers   d. neither his parents nor teachers

    2. In Egyptian society, if a child is not good at academics, his parents will ___.

        a. push him toward a university education regardless

        b. let him focus on what he shows promise in, be it sports or art

        c. often put him into a different school in hopes of improvement

        d. send him to summer school

    3. Which faculty is also considered prestigious for girls?

        a. nursing   c. teaching

        b. pharmacology   d. journalism

    4. Islam thinks that some university students are unsuccessful because ___.

        a. their field of study is too difficult for them

        b. they never actually wanted to study in that faculty

        c. their families do not support them

        d. they do not have enough time to study

5. Islam concludes by ___.

   a. thanking his parents for their support in his educational pursuits
   b. advising young people to resist the pressures from society and study what they love
   c. mentioning that he too wishes he had not studied engineering
   d. advising parents to let their children pursue the field they choose

Matching

MSA	ECA	English
أرادَ	عايْز	(not) at all
إلى أَيْنَ	النِّهارْدة	but
إمّا... و إمّا...	عنْدنا	don't make him
الآنَ	على فَيْن	dude; man
جَيِّد	دُوّت	either... or...
ذلكَ	أَيْه	good
على الإطْلاق	فيه	in our country
عنْدنا	كُوِّيس	not... anymore
كان يجِبُ علَيْكَ أنْ	بسّ	now
لا تجْعلْهُ	خلاص	that
لكِن	دِلْوقْتي	there is; there are
ما عادَ	ماعادْش	this
ما، ماذا	دِيّة	today
هذِه	يا عمّ	want
هُناكَ	يا إمّا... يا إمّا...	what
يا صديقي	يا رَيْتك	where to
اليَوْم	ما تْخلِّيهوش	you should have...

Answers

Main Idea: b **True or False:** 1. F[8-9] 2. T[18] 3. F[33] 4. T[38] 5. F[41-43] **Multiple Choice:** 1. c[12-13] 2. a[18] 3. b[34] 4. b[42] 5. d[45-46]
Matching: what أَيْه / ذلكَ that دُوّت / إلى أَيْنَ where to على فَيْن / عنْدنا in our country عنْدنا / اليَوْم today النِّهارْدة / أرادَ want عايْز
now الآنَ / دِلْوقْتي (not) at all على الإطْلاق / خلاص but لكِن / بسّ good جَيِّد / كُوِّيس هُناكَ there is; there are فيه / ما، ماذا
not... anymore ما عادَ / دِيّة this هذِه / يا عمّ dude; man يا صديقي / يا إمّا... يا إمّا...either... or... إمّا... و إمّا... / يا رَيْتك you should
have... كان يجِبُ علَيْكَ أنْ / ما تْخلِّيهوش don't make him لا تجْعلْهُ

Text

أهْلًا بِكُم.	1	Welcome.

اممم... كُنْت عايز أكلِّمكُم النَّهارْدة عن مَوْضوع بيخُصّ عنْدنا:	2	Um... I wanted to talk to you today about something that is of interest in our country:
نظرة النَّاس للمدارس والجامْعات أوْ للتعْليم عُمومًا.	3	people's view toward schools and colleges or education in general.
إحْنا عنْدنا قبْلَ ما الـ... اااه... ما الطِّفْل يِكون عنْدُه أيّ خلْفية عن أيّ حاجة،	4	In our country, ... before uh... a child has any background about anything,
طبْعًا الأب والأمّ هُمّ اِللي بيبْقوا مسْؤولين عن مسار حَياتُه في البِداية لِحدّ ما يِدْرك هُوَ رايِح على فَيْن.	5*	surely the father and the mother are the ones responsible for his life path in the beginning until he realizes where he is going.
فـ... عنْدنا غالِبية النَّاس بـ... اااه... دخلوا الطِّفْل دُوّت مرْحلة الحضانة وبعْدها مرْحلة الإبْتِدائية.	6	And... most people here put their children in nursery school then primary school.
وطبْعًا بيبْدأ تِتْضح معالِم الشَّخْص دُوّت أوْ الطِّفْل دُوّت في المرْحلة الإبْتِدائية.	7	And of course the characteristics of him, or of that child, become apparent during primary school.
تلاقيه مثلًا بعْدَ آخِر سنة لُه في المرْحلة الإبْتِدائية، تِبْدأ تبان علَيْه المعالِم،	8	For instance, by his last year in primary school, you'll find that these characteristics are showing in him.
يعْني هُوَ طالِب كُوِّيس، طالِب مِش كُوِّيس،	9	That is, is he a good student? Is he not a good student?
بيْذاكِر، ما بيْذاكِرْش.	10*	Does he study? Does he not study?
طبْعًا بيبْقى فيه جُزْء مِن ااااه... مِن الطِّفْل إنّ هُوَ مِشاغِب مثلًا	11	Surely, it's partly [because] of... uh... of the child, that he's naughty, for example,
بيبْقى فيه جُزْء مِن الأهْل إنّ هُمّ ما بِيراقْبوش.	12	partially because of his family, that they don't keep an eye on him,
فيه جُزْء مِن المُدرِّسين أوْ المسْؤولين في المدْرسة إنّ هُمّ ما بِيتابِعوش أوْ مُسْتَواهُم مِش كُوِّيس.	13	and partially because of the teachers and those responsible at school, that they don't monitor him or that they're not competent.
في كُلّ الأحْوال، يعْني إنّ أنا أحْيانًا ألاقي الطَّالِب دُوّت بعْدَ المرْحلة الإبْتِدائية مثلًا ساقِط... ساقِط، شال موادّ ااه... في ااه... السّنة السَّادسة لُه.	14	Anyway, I find that a student after primary school has failed... failed, he has failed the subjects, in uh... in his sixth year.
فلمَّا يِشيل موادّ ما أعْتقِدْش إنّ ده طالِب كُوِّيس، إنّهُ يِكمِّل في المرْحلة التّعْليمية.	15	When he has failed the subjects, then I don't think that he's a good student, that he'll finish his education.
هُوَ مُمْكِن مثلًا تلاقيه بيرْسِم كُوِّيس جِدًّا جِدًّا جِدًّا و... أوْ مثلًا بيلْعب كُرة كُوِّيس جِدًّا جِدًّا.	16	You might, for example, find that he is really, really, really good at drawing, and... or playing soccer,
فـ... ااااه... الأهْل ليه طالما هُمّ شايْفين إنّ هُوَ لُه موهِّبة في كُرة القدم، ااه... يِخْلوه يِكمِّل في كُرة القدم.	17	so his family, since they see he's gifted at soccer, will let him continue with soccer.
لأ، بسّ إحْنا عنْدنا المُجْتمع إنّ هُمّ بيْنظُروا للمرْحلة الإعْدادية اِللي هِيَ بعْدَ الإبْتِدائية مُباشرةً إنّ هِيَ مرْحلة تعْليمية مِتْقدِّمة ومكانة اِجْتماعية فيفضّل إنّ هُوَ يِكمِّل فيها.	18	But no, in our society the family sees preparatory school, which is immediately after primary school, as an advanced level of education and social position, so they prefer that he proceed with it.

بِقوم الطِّفْل ااه... خلاص دِلوقْتي ماعادْش طِفْل يَعْني إلى حدّ ما ااه... يُدخُل المرْحلة الإعْدادية ويكمّل فيها.	19	The child, okay, not a child anymore, you know, more or less, uh... he enters and pursues the preparatory school.
وبعْدَ ما يخلّص المرْحلة الإعْدادية ااه... تلات سنين، ييجي يُقْبل عنْدنا بعْدَ الإعْدادية فيه مجْموعة أقْسام:	20	And after he finishes preparatory school... three years, we have after preparatory school some departments,
فيه ثانَوي عامّ، فيه ثانَوي تُجاري، فيه ثانَوي صناعي وهكذا،	21	there is general secondary school, commercial secondary school, industrial secondary school, and so on.
وفيه ثانَوي تمْريض.	22	And there is nursing secondary school.
فطبْعًا مفْروض في ااه... تالْتة إعْدادي، الشّخص دوّت بيْحدِّد مساره،	23	So, during the third year of preparatory school, one has to choose his path.
بسّ برْضُه علشان هُوَ لسّه ما يْعيش المسْؤولية كامْلة فمفْروض الأهل في البَيْت بيْساعْدوه.	24	But so that he doesn't have the whole responsibility; the family at home helps him.
يقولوله: يا ابْني إنْتَ كُوِّس في أيْه؟ إنْتَ حابِب أيْه؟ إنْتَ مِش حابِب أيْه؟ إنْتَ نِفْسك تِكمّل في أيْه؟ وهكذا.	25	They ask him, "Son, what are you good at? What do you like? What don't you like? What path do you feel like following?" and so forth.
فالمفْروض يعْني إنّ الـ... ااه... الـ... الشّخص بيْختار المجال الِّلي هُوَ مُمْكِن يناسِبُه الِّلي هُوَ مُمْكِن يكون مُتفوّق فيه.	26	So, you know, uh... one is supposed to choose a field that it suited to him, that he can be successful at.
بسّ إحْنا علشان المُجْتمع عنْدنا بيْنْظر لكُلّيات مُعيّنة أوْ لمدارس مُعيّنة إنّ هِيَ دِيّة الأصْل، إنّ هِيَ دِيّة الشَّيْء الكُوِّس جِدًّا، النّظرة الجميلة.	27	But our society considers certain faculties or certain schools to be "the ones", the best thing, the right view.
فبالتّالي بيْحاوْلوا يوصّلوه للمكان ده.	28	Consequently, they try to help him reach that place.
فمُعْظم النّاس عنْدنا بيُدخُلوا ثانَوي عامّ.	29	Most people in our country go on to the general secondary school.
حتّى لَوْ كان هُمّ مُسْتواهُم ما يأهّلُهُمْش لِلثّانَوي العامّ برْضُه بيُدخُلوا ثانَوي عامّ.	30	Even if their level is not suitable to do so, they go into the general secondary school.
وبعْدَ ما يُدخُلوا ثانَوي عامّ فيه بعْدَ الثّانَوي العامّ طبْعًا مرْحلة الجامْعة.	31	And after they've gone into the general secondary school, of course after the general secondary school, there's the university level.
فإنْتَ لمّا تيجي على مرْحلة الجامْعة فيه كُلّيات كِثيرة جِدًّا.	32	And when you get to the university level, there are really a lot of faculties,
النّاس عنْدنا في الـ... في المُجْتمع ما يِعْرفوش غَيْر كُلّيتَيْن: كُلّية الهنْدسة وكُلّية الطِّب.	33	[but] people here in... in our society just know two of them: engineering and medicine.
أحْيانًا لمّا بيْبقى الأمْر مُرْتبِط بالبنات شُوّية يِكلّموا عن كُلّية الصَّيْدلة.	34	Sometimes when it comes to girls, they speak about the faculty of pharmacology.

لمّا تيجي تُذكُر كُلّية التّمريض: تَمريض أَيْه يا عمّ؟ تَمْريض مِش كُوِّيس.	35	[But] when you mention the faculty of nursing, [they say,] "What's nursing, dude? That's no good."
تيجي تُذكُر التِجارة: تِجارة أَيْه؟ يعْني حَيَطْلع يشْتغل أَيْه، مِش عارِف.	36	When you mention commerce, "What's commerce? What will he be doing [with that]? I don't know!"
بيُنْظُروا لِجميع الكُلّيات على إنّها حاجة مِش كُوِّيسة،	37	They look at all the faculties as if they were no good.
فتْلاقي كُلّ الطُّلّاب، أكْتر من تِسعين في المية من الطُّلّاب، بيِبْقى حاطِط عَيْنُه على حاجة واحْدة بس، إنّ هُوَ يُدْخُل يا إمّا هنْدسة يا إمّا يُدْخُل طِبّ... طِبّ.	38	You'll find that all students, over ninety percent of students, have their eye on one thing only, either to get into engineering or to get into medicine.
لَوْ ما دخلْش هنْدسة وما دخلْش طِبّ تلاقيه حاجة ااه... زعْلان جدًّا جدًّا ويائِس جدًّا،	39	If he doesn't get into engineering, and doesn't get into medicine, you'll find him uh... quite sad and depressed,
والجماعة في البَيْت بيْقولولُه يا رَيْتك كُنْت كُوِّيس، يا رَيْتك ذاكِرْت، يا رَيْتك، يا رَيْتك.	40	and everyone at home will tell him, "If only you'd been better, you should've studied, you should've, you should've..."
وبعْدَ ما بيُدْخُل الـ... الجامْعة، فلْنِفْرِض مثلًا يعْني جدلًا إنّ هُوَ دخل هنْدسة أوْ دخل طِبّ،	41	Then after he gets into... university, let's suppose, for example, for the sake of argument that he got into engineering or medicine,
تِلاقيه طالِب فاشِل جدًّا جدًّا لأنّ هُوَ ما كانْش راغِب في المجال دُوت.	42	you'd find that he's a really, really unsuccessful student because he never wanted to be in this field.
لا كان راغِب لا في الهنْدسة ولا كان راغِب في الطِّبّ.	43	He neither wanted engineering nor did he want medicine.
فأنا كُنْت أتمنّى مِن المُجتمع إنّ هُوَ يُحسّن النّظرة شْوية.	44	So I was hoping that society would improve its perspective somewhat.
إنْتَ شايِف الطّالِب دُوّة كُوِّيس في المجال دُوّة، خلاص تخلّيه يكمّل في المجال دُوّة.	45	[If] you notice that a student is good in a certain field, then fine, let him pursue that field.
ما تْخلّيهوش يِروح مجال تاني هُوَ مِش حابِبُه أوْ مِش راغِب فيه.	46	Don't make him go into another field that he doesn't like or doesn't want to be in.
دي حاجة صُغيّرة كِده عن المُجتمع عنْدنا وبإذْن الله حتِتْحسّن في المُسْتَقْبِل القريب.	47	[So,] that was just a little something about our society here and, God willing, it will be improve soon.
أتمنّى يكون عنْدكُم المَوْضوع ده مُخْتلِف عن كِده.	48	I hope the situation is different from this in your country.
يلّا سلام.	49	Good-bye.

Notes

*5 The 3rd person masculine prefix يـ is usually dropped when the present tense prefix بـ is added. The 3rd person plural suffix is ـوا -ū (MSA: ـونَ).

*10 The negative is formed by sandwiching a verb (or particle) with ما...ش.

notes

lingualism

Visit our website for information on current and upcoming titles,

free excerpts, and language learning resources.

www.lingualism.com

Printed in Great Britain
by Amazon